Praise for Jenna Qu

"Jenna Quinn's story bravely explores the damage child sexual abuse wreaks on children, families, and communities. Few stories have so clearly demonstrated the deep and crucial role of Children's Advocacy Centers—like the one that served Jenna and her family—in offering healing, justice, and trust in a system that works. This powerful narrative will inspire empathy in parents, families, teachers, classmates, and friends of victims and inspire hope in survivors that, like Jenna, they can heal and, in turn, help protect children from abuse."

—Teresa Huizar, Executive Director, National Children's Alliance

"With honesty and grace, Jenna Quinn has done a masterful job describing her remarkable journey of pain, healing, and forgiving. In so many ways she clearly demonstrates the need for faith communities to understand, prevent, and properly address the horror of child sexual abuse. Jenna's life story confirms how important it is for faith communities to welcome, support, and unconditionally love those who have been abused. You will find here a memoir of exceptional courage, faith, and hope."

—Boz Tchividjian, Executive Director of GRACE and
Professor of Law, Liberty University School of Law

"A masterful account of, a far too common story, how a child from a loving and caring family becomes a victim of sexual abuse by a trusted adult. Jenna's story demonstrates the extraordinary resilience and strength of children to overcome abuse and how, from being a victim, Jenna became a powerful champion and tireless voice for child sexual abuse prevention."

—Dr. Joanna Rubinstein, President and CEO,
World Childhood Foundation USA

"From child victim to survivor to renowned advocate, Jenna Quinn has changed the landscape of child safety in schools across Texas. She is a hero and a courageous voice advocating for change. Jenna's Law was the first of its kind to mandate that teachers, parents, and students be made aware of the signs of child sexual abuse and be ready to respond. We applaud the work she continues today to champion stronger, more comprehensive legislation centered around prevention education."

—Lyndon Haviland, MPH, DrPH, CEO,
Darkness to Light (D2L)

"Captivating and refreshingly humorous at times—I couldn't put this book down. Jenna does an exquisite job of providing insight into her darkest trials of trauma and through the road to health, happiness, and victory. This book inspirationally addresses a dark topic and shows the reader, with sensitivity, how predators work. Jenna's passion to give children a voice and her heart behind passing Jenna's law is one that deserves the highest praise. This prevention tool is a must read and a job well done."

—Stacie Rumenap, President of Stop Child Predators

"*Pure In Heart* is a must read. This book can give courage, hope, and support to anyone. Jenna inspires survivors to reach out for supportive help, and know that they are not defined by their past. This book is more than inspirational. It's eye-opening and gives the reader a guide to prevention. Through Jenna's transparency she shares a gift of herself, her hurt, fear, and shame. She also shares her spiritual victory, humor, and joy. What more could we ask of a writer? I highly recommend that it is read and discussed by all."

—Michael Medoro, Chief Development Officer of Childhelp

PURE
In Heart

A Memoir of Overcoming Abuse and Passing Jenna's Law

Jenna Quinn, MS

Liberty House Publishing
DALLAS, TEXAS

Published by
Liberty House Publishing

Some names and identifying details have been changed to protect the privacy of individuals and reader sensitivity. The conversations in the book all come from the author's recollections, though they are not written to represent word-for-word transcripts unless otherwise noted. Rather, the author has retold them in a way that evokes the feeling and meaning of what was said and, in all instances, the essence of the dialogue is accurate.

Scripture quotations are from the ESV® Bible (The Holy Bible, English Standard Version®), copyright © 2001 by Crossway, a publishing ministry of Good News Publishers. Used by permission. All rights reserved.

Library of Congress Number: 2016917641

ISBN: 978-0-692-73872-6

Cover and interior design: Gary A. Rosenberg
Cover photograph: Alli Pratt. Apodo Photography

Printed in the United States of America

Behold,
the Lord's hand is not shortened,
that it cannot save,
or his ear dull,
that it cannot hear.

—Isaiah 59:1 (ESV)

FOREWORD

Childhood trauma and sexual abuse happens more often than anybody wants to believe. In the United States, one in three girls and one in six boys are sexually abused before the age of eighteen. Of these children, 93 percent know their attacker and many will never disclose their abuse to anyone. Less than 12 percent of all child sexual abuse is ever reported.

These numbers are startling, sobering, and horrific. Because the initial trauma of abuse is so life changing, the ability to demonstrate resilience in the face of trauma is nothing short of miraculous. In this book, Jenna Quinn shares her strength and a drive to protect others from the long-term effects and outcomes of abuse that she experienced firsthand.

Pure In Heart tells the compelling, unforgettable, unique, and sometimes humorous story of a soft-spoken young girl, Jenna Quinn, who overcame three years of child sexual abuse at the will of a trusted family friend and basketball coach while attending a private Christian school. Jenna struggles with the abuse and falls into a deep depression while managing post-traumatic stress, social withdrawal, and a complete crisis of her faith.

With the help of her two sisters, Jenna is able to tell her family and end the abuse. Despite her abuser being part of her close-knit school community, or perhaps because of it, Jenna receives little support from her school after she tells. At sixteen years old, she finds herself packing her bags for a mental institution with no hope of a normal life until she is released. Facing her senior year in high school, Jenna has critical choices to make as her family prepares to go to trial. In *Pure In Heart,* Jenna shares how she starts on her road to recovery and healing that eventually leads her to her greatest passion: helping protect other children from the horrors of child sexual abuse.

Jenna's story answers the uncomfortable questions people have about child sexual abuse: How can a family not see the abuse? How can a child keep silent for years? What resources and skills can we teach to children to help them prevent or end abuse by speaking up?

This book is not just a memoir, it's also a training tool with prevention as the hallmark. Jenna wrote this book intentionally to raise awareness for social change and with hopes of true healing and freedom for those who have been victimized.

There are an unfathomable 42 million survivors of child sexual abuse estimated in America. Jenna Quinn is a rare survivor in that her extraordinary courage is helping children who have been sexually abused.

Jenna found the courage to actively engage politicians in the Texas State Legislature to pass the first child sexual abuse education law named after a survivor in the state of Texas, and in the United States. Jenna's Law requires that each school district adopt and implement a prevention policy that educates students, teachers, and parents on the likely warning signs of sexual abuse. It also addresses actions a child who is a victim should take to obtain intervention and available counseling options for students affected.

Pure In Heart is destined to be a critical read for survivors, parents, and child safety advocates worldwide. Jenna's tenacity in passing Jenna's Law legislation is a giant leap forward in the battle to protect America's children. Her vigor in sharing her story to spare others the torment she endured has led a national movement for schools across the United States.

Jenna travels nationwide to speak to a variety of audiences, and she continues to inspire and encourage other survivors on a personal level. She partners with non-profits to raise awareness in their communities, and speaks to legislative officials about prevention laws. Her life shows what can happen when an ordinary girl follows a passion birthed from great pain. Jenna's story embodies the human spirit and will touch your life in a way few books can.

Benah J. Parker, PhD
National Director of Prevention Education, Childhelp
Childhelp Speak Up Be Safe

CHAPTER 1

Even as a young adolescent, I had plans for the future—an honor student looking forward to graduating high school and going on to attend a major university of my choice. Now I felt helpless to see that anything good could happen in my life. My parents' assurance that I could do anything I set my mind to no longer held meaning for me.

These past few months I hardly slept. And whether I was awake or asleep, it seemed I was living in a nightmare. Even the sleeping medication my psychiatrist prescribed for me didn't work well. All too often I watched the sun come up. Each morning, I dragged myself out of bed and thought about skipping school. Then my thoughts would return to how much my parents sacrificed to send me to a prestigious private school, and how I had already disappointed them in so many ways as a result of my changed attitude and personality. Sparing them more disappointment was usually enough to get me up and ready for school.

I dressed in my traditional plaid uniform skirt and oversized hoodie—not giving any extra thought to how I looked. *What was the point of trying to look good for anyone?* For years, it was a struggle to act normal. I did the best I could. I knew I was a big phony, imitating the words and actions of my friends—each day just trying to keep my head above water. I just needed to hang on a little longer until the end of the school year in May.

Today was not an unusual day in many ways. My teacher and all my classmates knew that I had become a nut case: someone to be avoided, if possible. When I drove to school and parked my car in its designated spot I sat for a few minutes staring at the once friendly bare walls of the school building while an overwhelming sense of oppression overcame me.

Finally, I opened my car door and nearly tripped with my first step. Right away I could hear my feet dragging on the pavement as I walked the short distance from my car to the school. As I trudged on, it flashed through my mind that only earlier this year I was nominated to the Homecoming Court. It seemed so long ago. My classmates witnessed me lose any last ounce of joy left in me. It used to be that, when I walked, I bounced, earning the nickname "Tigger." Now, compared to only a few months ago, I was a nonfunctioning zombie who walked the school hallways with my head hung low, eyes downcast, and made little eye contact with anyone. There was no life or bounce left in me.

As with most days, today I just wanted to get into my first period class without having to give another disingenuous smile or fake a real conversation. Walking through the halls of the school I felt deep loneliness, emptiness, and rejection from the top of my head to the end of my toes. Insidious guilt controlled my heart and soul. The amount of pain I felt was heavier than my load of books. I couldn't imagine a worse place to be.

When the school bell rang for my first class, I was already seated in my desk. As I pulled out a blank piece of paper for the quiz, I felt a wave of nausea and fatigue pass through my whole body.

I struggled to hold back the queasiness while my teacher handed out the quizzes. Trying to hold it all inside, I felt myself making strange faces. A classmate noticed and, with a startled look on her face, asked, "Are you OK?" Everyone in the classroom glanced my way. I felt their stares. I couldn't take it. I scrambled up from my desk and rushed out the door, almost making it to the commode in time. My teacher followed me out the door to see what was wrong.

She looked at the mess and looked at me. In a perturbed tone she said, "Are you OK? Did you throw up?"

"I feel queasy," is all I could murmur.

Embarrassed, and thinking all the time that I should finish my quiz, I struggled to my feet off the restroom floor. Bent over, thinking I must look like the Hunchback of Notre Dame, I stumbled back to the classroom. My hand was on the schoolroom doorknob when my teacher called out, "Ooh no, you're going straight to the nurse! Stay right here."

She brought my heavy backpack to me and laid it on the floor beside me while saying, "OK, Jenna Quinn, let's go. You'll get your quiz after I make a new version for you. But for now, you'll see the school nurse." Reading my face, which must have showed a look of defeat, she said, "Don't worry, you'll take the quiz, because you *need* to pass it. You're already on the verge of failing." I fought back tears. Surely she knew I was already aware of my academic problems. The last thing I needed was summer school. *How am I going to explain this to Mom,* I thought.

Although I was released from school to go home, it didn't bring me much relief. I was missing important classes. During the short drive home my eyes welled with tears at what my life had become. I wasn't the little girl my parents, Kellie and Greg Quinn, raised. I hadn't seen her in years. When I parked the car in front of the house it took all the energy I had to lug my backpack inside and up the stairs to my room.

When I walked into my room and collapsed on my bed, my first thought was, *Maybe if I fall asleep for long enough, I'll wake up to a different life.* After taking an antianxiety pill prescribed by my psychiatrist, I was asleep within minutes and slept until late afternoon. When I awoke, I noticed missed calls on my cell phone from both Mom and Dad. The office called them, so they knew I was sent home early.

Through all this, and for many reasons, I couldn't bring myself to tell my parents or what seemed like a whole busload of medical professionals what was *really* happening. I couldn't muster up the courage to tell anyone, and I wasn't strong enough to solve the problem on my own. The only time I felt a glimmer of hope was when I prayed at night, which wasn't often anymore.

In desperation, Mom and Dad felt they only had one other option. They called my psychiatrist, who informed them he would make the necessary arrangements at Green Oaks Mental Hospital.

Later that evening, the three of us, Mom, Dad, and myself, sat on the couch while they explained, again, why this action was necessary. They said it would probably be temporary. After a long silence, while I fought to hold back my tears, I hugged them both and ran to my room. I threw myself upon my bed and let the tears flow.

CHAPTER 2

Growing up I had a strong sense of self, which was always enforced by the actions of my parents. They raised three girls with gentle, but firm, discipline, setting a Christian-based example for us to follow. Mom stayed home with us for most of our early childhood years.

She kept us busy with Bible devotionals, making crafts, baking, and organized sports. At the end of each day, she read to us and we said our prayers. I enjoyed curling my fingers through her long blonde hair and watching her piercing blue eyes' expressions as she read. Then, she tucked us in and kissed us good night.

I was the middle sister, and as early as I can remember I had always been known as the "Peacemaker." Stephanie, my older sister, had the most natural bossy tendencies and was usually the first to inform Mom about everything. She was tall, lean, and had big brown eyes. Her skin was fair, and she had straight dark hair.

Lauren, my younger sister, had loud, natural attention-gaining tendencies. She was shorter and muscular for her age. She also had big, brown eyes with fair skin and the curliest dark hair I had ever seen. Sometimes Steph teased Lauren and told her that she would eat her hair, causing Lauren to cry. She had perfect ringlets, and it constantly reminded us of the curly fries we loved eating so much.

My looks resembled Mom more with lighter, thinner hair, a larger smile, and teeth I hadn't grown into yet. As a natural observer, I was constantly entertained while growing up with my sisters.

I was close to both Stephanie and Lauren and shared a room with each of them at different times during my childhood. Stephanie and I are three years apart, and Lauren and I are four years apart. Since there is a seven-year difference between Stephanie and Lauren, they didn't have much in common. I learned how to speak on each of their "levels" as the "peacemaker" and quickly came to the conclusion that I should not add any fuel to the fire.

Sometimes at night, after family dinners, my sisters and I performed "shows" for my parents. We were in ballet classes and used every excuse to put on our leotards and twirl. I mostly remember my older sister instructing me on exactly everything I needed to do for our routines. "No, don't twirl that way, twirl the other way," Stephanie said. We turned the lights out, made Dad hold up a spotlight and shine the light on us as we marched around the corner of the living room one by one, lined up after each other. Dad was always patient with us and went with the flow, accepting our theatrical music choices. His laugh was contagious and because of it we twirled around faster during our performances.

Almost every day was dress up for me because Stephanie enjoyed braiding my hair and fixing my outfits. Sometimes she was so rough when she brushed my hair I got upset, at which she would reply, "Beauty is pain."

As a six-year-old, beauty was next to the last thing on my mind, and I often reminded her of that. I mostly wanted to skip "dress up" and ride bikes, climb trees, and catch bugs and any other critters that moved in my path. Mainly we caught salamanders, garden snakes, and tadpoles. We were a family of animal lovers. Some of this love we gained from Mom's stories of her adventures with animals while growing up on a ranch in Colorado.

We always had cats and dogs as pets. Some of the other animals seemed to come and go quickly, dying off or running away. I liked to keep the fish tank full with tadpoles we caught from the creek behind our house. We never had just one animal, but at least two for each daughter. We had almost every household pet known to man at any given time including bunnies, hamsters, hermit crabs, birds, snakes, and horses.

On the weekends in the summer, taking a bike ride with Dad was my favorite activity. We lived near a snow cone stand within biking distance, so we often biked to it to treat ourselves to a cold summer snack. Sometimes Dad and I doubled up together and rode on a bright yellow, two-seated bike.

Even as a small child, church was my favorite place to visit. Although I didn't understand or relate much to what the preacher said, there was always singing as well as dancing in the aisles in a few of the churches we attended. To this day I remember one specific moment clearly. I was lying on my bed thumbing through the pictures in my Children's Bible when I stopped on the page where Jesus was on the cross. Mom talked about this event many times, but I never had a clear view of it in my mind. After reading what I could about the crucifixion, I looked again at the picture and cried. A minute or two passed before I recovered enough to say aloud in a whisper, "I'm sorry, Jesus." I ran downstairs and told Mom what I saw in my Bible. I wanted to give my life to Jesus that minute, and Mom helped me through the experience.

By the time I started second grade, Mom accepted a fourth-grade teaching position at a private Christian school, enrolling all three of us girls and taking us with her each morning.

At first I was afraid of a new school and what it would be like to make new friends. When we went with Mom to a special uniform store to be fitted for school clothes, I knew right then it was a bad idea—they were stiff and uncomfortable. Mom assured us they would feel different after they were "broke in," which I believed about as much as I did when the nurse told me before my second vaccination shot that it wouldn't hurt.

Maybe Mom felt our apprehension at changing schools, because the days before school started she talked a lot about the superior education opportunities available to us, including learning about God's Word each and every day in class. And, she said, "It will be a safe place for you."

My experiences at the new private Christian school would change my life in a way that no one could have imagined.

CHAPTER 3

My nervousness started in the morning on the first day of school when I had to put on my newly bought, stiff, plaid jumper uniform. Stephanie did my hair that morning and put extra hairspray in my braided ponytail. As usual, her zest with the hairspray made me cough. Because Mom was a teacher now, we had to arrive at school early. Steph and I helped Mom put the finishing touches on her classroom before her students arrived. Unlike me, my sister didn't seem nervous at all.

As I left the room for my class, Mom leaned down, kissed my forehead, and whispered, "Honey, I'm just right down the hallway if you need anything. Come and get me. I love you." I was early to class the first day and every day. I felt hopeful when I found my desk first before the other students and could observe my classmates enter our classroom. I said, "Hi" and waved at each student as they came in. Most said "Hi" back. My teacher looked like she was about one hundred years old and most of us were afraid of her.

As we got into a routine at the new school we met our school secretary, Grace Russell, and her son Jake and daughter Jackie. Jake and Jackie were in the same grades as Stephanie and me. They lived a short distance from us and our school schedules were similar. Grace's husband, Mark Russell, worked someplace outside the school system.

Grace always smiled at me, and her big blue eyes lit up when she saw me. Her blonde hair was extremely short above her neck, and she fit the role of a secretary well. Jake and Jackie looked almost identical. They both had bright, blue eyes, with fair complexions, but Jake had brown hair and Jackie had blonde hair.

Our private school was small, consisting of about fifty students in my entire grade, compared to my former public school, which was much larger. Most teachers, students, and parents knew all about one another and their families. And so it was that I knew all about Jake before we became close friends. Jake and I often saw each other after school while waiting for our moms to finish work. We also found ways to amuse ourselves to pass the time at Stephanie and Jackie's volleyball games. Jake and I were not in the same classroom together, but we shared the same classes/subjects and similar homework. Sometimes we did our homework together at games. If we didn't want to work on homework together, we found other fun ways to entertain ourselves.

At the volleyball games we often stole volleyballs and had two-person games on the sidelines or under the bleachers. People in the stands knew that our families were close and that we were siblings of the team members. It didn't matter that Jake was a boy. I grew up with mostly male cousins, and he had a sister. So, we were both comfortable around the opposite sex. What mattered is that we enjoyed each other's company. Through my idyllic friendship with Jake I met his father, Mark Russell.

My family and the Russell family both attended all the volleyball and basketball games at the school. Neither family ever missed a game. Since the Russells were a big part of the cheering section (they made the most noise), we ended up sitting together.

As the Russell and Quinn friendship grew, our families discovered we had much in common. Dad and Mr. Russell were both businessmen and former college athletes. Mom and Grace sat together at games and could be heard above the whole stadium cheering section, and both loved to talk about their children.

It didn't take long for the two families to form a mutually trusting friendship. As the years passed, the Quinn and Russell families became almost as one family.

"We're going to Disney World!" I shouted to no one in particular, as we pulled away from our house. We were off to Florida with the Russells, caravan style. This was my first time to go to Disney World. Stephanie and I couldn't wait to ride all of the rides and see the Disney Princesses in person.

I had just finished fifth grade, and now I was looking forward to a fun-filled summer. *Could it get any better than Disney World?* I rode with Dad in the van along with Mr. Russell and Jake. Since Mr. Russell talked a lot, Jake and I decided to watch as many movies as we could throughout the trip. As soon as one movie ended, Jake and I blurted out, "How many more movies until we get there?"

When we finally arrived at Disney World, I thought my eyes would pop out of my head with each step I took toward the park. Everywhere I looked, there was something that caught my attention. As we waited for rides, I was about as patient as any kid could be during their first visit to Disney World—not at all patient.

While waiting in line for a park ride, a little girl in a wheelchair rolled over Mr. Russell's foot. Hopping around on one foot, he shouted at the little girl, "Watch where you're going! Can't you see?" She immediately apologized, but he continued to stare at her with rage showing in his face as she wheeled away. I was so uncomfortable with all of this and would have occasion to relate this incident to his character many times in the future.

We all went to the beach the next day. Mr. Russell carried his camera with him at all times. He snapped pictures of our families together, of all the trees, buildings, the ocean and, it seemed to me, everything else no one would ever care to see again.

Jake and I were building sandcastles on the beach when Mr. Russell appeared with his camera. He took several pictures of us, then stood around and watched for a while. I was sitting straddle-legged on the beach, working on our sandcastle when Jake got on his feet and said he was going to go wading. And that was fine by me. Jake wasn't focused enough on building sandcastles, anyway.

I got up on my knees and sort of ignored Mr. Russell, thinking he would follow Jake to the water. It was then he walked closer to me and snapped several pictures of me in my bikini while I worked on the sandcastle. At first I didn't take much notice to his picture-taking antics, moving around, taking shots at different angles. I had to maintain the structure of my castle. *Why would anyone want to see so many pictures of me building a sandcastle?* It didn't make any sense at all. As time passed and

Jake hadn't returned, I started getting uncomfortable, especially when Mr. Russell stopped taking pictures and started moving his eyes up and down my body.

I was getting to my feet when Mr. Russell remarked, "You're such a pretty girl." I didn't understand any of this. I just knew something was wrong, and I had to get away from it all. I looked toward the beach and saw Jake still in the water. Probably, he was not coming back to help me on the sandcastle.

When I was firmly on my feet, Mr. Russell said, "Smile, pretty girl" as he snapped another picture of me. Turning away, I walked as fast as I could to my parents, a short distance from where we were.

CHAPTER 4

Seventh grade was my favorite, over all my other years in school. That was the year I felt I was truly "coming into being." Ambitious, I tried out for all the sports that were offered, with more enthusiasm for my two favorites—basketball and volleyball.

After trying out, I was accepted into the more advanced eighth-grade basketball team. I could tell Dad was so proud, and pleasing him in sports meant everything to me. Dad was a college athlete, and I felt that it was important for me to carry on his athletic legacy. Playing above my grade level really challenged me and made me want to be my very best.

Academically, I was also doing well. And it was no surprise to my parents that my favorite subject was Bible class. I don't know how my teacher chose who won the award, but I must have showed a diligence to learn the Bible and apply it because I received the "Bible Student" award for the year. It caused a huge celebration in our house.

Physically, I grew tall and lean, developing at a normal age— not too early and not too late. My legs grew, my face thinned, and my smile stood out more. Filling out in all the right places,

JENNA QUINN

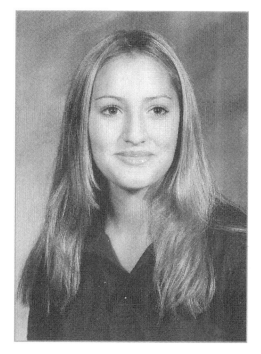

Jenna at age 14.

I could wear some of Stephanie's clothes, and this made me feel grown-up.

It was quickly obvious that Mr. Russell also noticed my growth spurt because he paid special attention to me. He went out of his way to make sure my family and I were comfortable around him, while building trust along the way. He attended and watched all of my basketball games, even when Jake wasn't playing. He often praised me, remarking that I had "great talent," and that I was "naturally athletic." He also told me I was "beautiful," and "special."

Since I was used to hearing encouragement like this from my grandparents and parents, and Mr. Russell was like an extension of the family, his praise didn't seem out of character. Instead, we

15

all assumed that he was treating me as if I was one of his daughters because, to our knowledge, he was a good father and a good husband. We were a tight little family, the Russells and the Quinns.

It wasn't long before slight physical touches accompanied Mr. Russell's verbal praises. As my family and I waited in the bleachers for the Varsity games to start, he occasionally got out of his seat, walked in front of me, placed his hand on my knee, leaned forward, and asked harmless questions about my day. Other times, he asked me if I wanted any food, and sometimes he asked me about basketball.

His physical gravitation grew in frequency, and it seemed he always found a warm way to greet me with a touch. My parents showed us lots of affection growing up, so it wasn't alarming. We all overlooked the way he found opportunities to be near me.

As time passed I focused more on playing basketball than anything else. I found the eighth grade coursework during my spring semester was difficult. Jake was my greatest help in subjects such as math and science. Since Jake was helping me, I often studied and completed my homework at the Russell's house after school. Jake and I worked out a routine each week, and that routine made my workload less arduous.

Every day after school, Grace drove Jake and me to their home. Since Mom worked later into the evenings, leaving school earlier was a bonus. Stephanie and Jackie had basketball practice or track practice every day after school, so Jake and I had the house to ourselves.

Once we arrived at the Russell's home, Jake and I raided the refrigerator for snacks. While we ate, we sometimes listened to music in the kitchen or watched TV before starting on homework. After homework we had a choice of various activities: playing basketball outside in the driveway; watching a movie; playing a round of pool; or swimming. The Russell's home had more amenities and activity options than our home. Sometimes Jake's dad was not home until later in the evening, and Mom picked me up after her lesson plans were finished.

During the days when Stephanie and I were both at the Russell's house in the evening, we usually shared dinner with them. Mr. Russell always gave an affectionate hug and kiss to Grace after arriving home from work. Then he usually remarked upon his pleasure at having our company. At the dinner table he was engaged and interested in learning about everyday school activities. He laughed if we told funny stories and congratulated us on good grades. The Russells seemed so happy and content. It was a picture perfect family setting, with plenty of laughter, story telling, and love.

The seemingly picture-perfect image of the Russells came to a screeching halt during the spring of my eighth grade year when Mr. Russell drove me home one evening after spending time with Jake. On the drive home Mr. Russell stopped at a stop sign, cleared his throat, and looked over at me. "You know you're very special to me and I'd do anything for you." I was silent and didn't really care too much about what he was getting at. "You're a good kid, I can tell, and your parents have done a good job of sheltering you. Are there any boys at school you like?"

After this he was silent and waited for a reaction out of me. While looking out the window I said, "I'm not into anyone." He continued on route to my house and asked more questions. "You know I can tell you all about how to have a relationship with a boy. I'd already had great experiences at your age." Then he started to go into detail about his past sexual relationships. I couldn't believe what I was hearing. By the time I processed what was being said, I had heard too much.

When he parked the car in front of my house, I cut him off mid-sentence. "I don't think that's OK to talk about." He cleared his throat and raised his brow. He always did this when he was perturbed. Then with ease in his voice he said, "It's just a conversation, relax darling." At that moment he leaned over the console and kissed me on the cheek. I pulled away from him and stepped out of the car as quickly as I could.

What happened in the car felt seriously wrong. At the same time, I didn't want to make a big fuss about it. Although the details of what he said were embarrassing, there was no physical harm done, so I ignored it the best I could, choosing to focus on better things.

Just a few short months later I was at the Russells again one evening. Jake and I decided to order Chinese food, rent an action movie (Jake's choice this time), and watch it in the front living room. We were the only ones who watched the movie, and by the time the movie ended Jake had fallen asleep on the couch.

The room was still dark as the movie credits played. I picked up their house phone to call Dad and ask him to pick me up. As I lifted up the phone, Mr. Russell walked into the living room.

He looked at me and said, "I don't mind taking you home. Tell your dad that I'm awake and he's probably half asleep already. You don't want to wake him up and *make* him drive you when you live right around the corner."

It appeared that Mr. Russell stayed up in the main living room area watching TV while everyone else was asleep. We were all tired because we had spent the afternoon swimming. I put the phone down and said, "No, it's OK, and my dad won't have a problem with picking me up."

I picked up the phone, again, and dialed home as I looked out the window. Mr. Russell moved toward me and stood so close that he could hear the phone conversation. Dad sounded as though he *was* half asleep already. Stepping closer to me, now, Mr. Russell interrupted our phone conversation to insist on taking me home. Dad didn't see any reason to refuse his thoughtful offer. Feeling tired, I agreed with my two father figures and told Dad that I would be home soon.

As Mr. Russell drove me home, he spoke first. He seemed to be more energetic than usual. "Well, did you have fun tonight?" After finishing a yawn I said, "Yeaaah." He promptly spoke again and in a more serious tone asked, "Are you dating anyone?"

I didn't respond. *Why did he care?* Then, he asked what I thought about Jake, his son. "Jake and I are good friends," I said. "He's like a brother to me," I added.

After checking on my relationship status and interest, he changed the subject to something that seemed to be more important to him. As he parked the car in front of our house, he looked at me and said, "You know that you're a beautiful girl don't you? I'm really surprised Jake doesn't take more interest in you. You're smart, beautiful, and athletic. You two look like a perfect couple."

"It's as I told you, Jake and I are just friends. Besides, I'm too young to take boys so seriously."

"You're not too young to do anything you don't want to do. Don't you ever think about kissing boys, or even more?"

At that time something came over me that I had never experienced. My chest tightened, and a sinking, dreadful feeling overcame my whole upper body. It was hard to breathe. Something here wasn't right. I could barely mutter the words, "Thank you for the ride home," while reaching for the seat belt buckle.

He quickly moved to my side of the car and pinned me to the seat, moving his hands all over me. Speaking with all the breath I had left, I said, "Stop, I can't breathe." It didn't matter how much I protested, whimpered, begged, or tried to push him away. He was strong and determined to have his way, but finally yielded to my pleas, threatening, "Don't you dare tell anyone about this. It would tear all our families apart, cause you to drop out of school, and who knows what other bad things would come of it."

Stumbling to the door dragging my backpack I straightened my clothes and hair the best I could before placing my key in the lock. My body was shaking all over, exhausted, my mind racing, trying to figure out a way to get by Dad and up to my room without him knowing something was terribly wrong with me.

Dad was on the couch, expecting me. He had questions. What movie had we watched, and a couple of other things that I could barely hear. I ignored his questions. Instead of answering, I said, "I'm tired. Can't we talk tomorrow?" and stumbled up the stairs to my room.

Once safe in my room, I threw myself upon the bed and tried to breathe normally while feeling numb, confused, and totally exhausted. I felt my body, but my brain was off somewhere else.

Mixed with other confusing emotions, a clammy, dirty feeling overcame me. I sat up in bed, knowing I had to take a shower that moment.

After showering and scrubbing myself like never before, I collected my thoughts the best I could. *What just happened?* I felt a terrible wrongness so deep that it seemed there was nothing I could do to rid myself of it. No amount of showering could help. I wanted to run downstairs and blurt it all out to Dad. *No! He will kill Mr. Russell, and, then, what will happen to Dad?* The shame, guilt, and humiliation were overwhelming. In my mind I kept repeating to myself: "It will never happen again." Sometime during the night I must have slept because I awoke to a bright, sunny room. I could hear voices downstairs. My first thought was: *How could something like that happen to me?*

At first, I couldn't go downstairs and face my family with such dirty feelings of shame, worthlessness, and self-blame running through my head. I even doubted myself that it happened in the first place, and I kept telling myself, over and over again, "It won't happen again."

I felt so confused. I didn't know what to tell my parents, or if I should tell them. *Will they even believe me, with the Russells being such good friends and Christians? What will Stephanie think? What will Jake and Jackie think?* I didn't want Jake to think anything less of his father or blame me for what happened. But worst of all, Mr. Russell threatened bad things would happen if I told.

In my guilty, confused, devastated, fearful, and disbelieving state of mind, I decided not to say anything. I didn't want to cause any dissention among my family and the Russells. Our families were too close for me to even consider such a thing. I almost changed my mind and blurted the whole thing out after my parents greeted me in the kitchen that Sunday morning. But I didn't.

Our two families were going to church together after breakfast. I felt too ashamed to even talk to God about what happened. Instead, I tried to hide it. *Maybe I did something to bring it on.* At church I only prayed it would never happen again. I kept a smiling face for Sunday, and tried to "get over it" the best I could while wanting to duck down and disappear. My goal was to forget all about it and hope that no one could see the ugly feelings of wrongness deep inside. But the harder I pushed it from my mind, the stronger my racing thoughts became. The most powerful thought that I couldn't push out of my mind was, *What if I can't block this out?*

CHAPTER 5

Playing sports was a year-round activity for me—volleyball in the fall, basketball in the winter, and cross-country in the spring. Out of all these sports, basketball was the one I practiced and played competitively off-season. My summers were spent at basketball practices, games, and tournaments because the most competitive players played in the off-season leagues. I grew to be very competitive. I tried out for a Junior Olympic team the summer after my eighth-grade year and made it.

Making a Junior Olympic team afforded me the opportunity to go to Australia for two weeks to play in tournaments with the other Junior Olympic team members. It was the experience of a lifetime. Having the opportunity to go to Australia and play in competitive basketball tournaments was a huge, earned privilege and, at the same time, a little intimidating for me. I was grateful that Stephanie, Jackie, and one of my closest friends, Erica, who was a year younger than me, also made the team. Stephanie and I worked extremely hard to raise money and get sponsors to help us pay for the two-week trip, so grueling basketball practices and fund-raising consumed the rest of my summer.

At the end of one of our practices, I overheard Jackie and Stephanie talking about the trip. Jackie said, "I think my dad is going to help chaperone and coach." I stopped in my tracks with the ball, mid-dribble. This was the opportunity of a lifetime for me. The chance for an experience like this may never come my way again. I didn't waver in my decision to go and I didn't want to make a fuss about it either.

Erica and I were "roomies" during the trip to Australia, and otherwise depended on each other like sisters throughout the whole experience. She was easygoing, fun to be around, and loved basketball as much as I did. Our second week of games was played in beautiful Cairns. We had one day during this week when no games were scheduled, so our team took the bus to the beach for the day.

Everyone on the team was soaking up the sun, playing in the waves, or trying to learn to surf for the first time. Erica and I decided that we wanted a little privacy, and we put a bit of distance between us and the rest of the team. We walked about fifty yards down the coast, still in sight from where everyone else played in the ocean. We set up our towels, laid out in our bikinis, and soaked up the warm rays of the sun. Lying on my stomach, I was almost asleep about 30 minutes later.

Urgently, Erica nudged me, "Hey, don't look now, but Mr. Russell is over there taking pictures of us."

"What? Are you being serious?"

As I looked over, I saw him walking towards us. Erica asked, "Why is he coming over here? Are we too far from the group?"

In almost a whisper I said, "I don't think so. Everyone else can see us."

We tried to get away by moving farther down the beach, but he followed. My feelings of relaxation quickly changed to trepidation.

Mr. Russell walked up, holding his camera. He grinned and

took more pictures of us as he made light, nonsense conversation: "You girls look like you're having fun. Why don't you smile for me, and I can send you the pictures?"

I rose up on one elbow and looked him straight in the eyes, "We don't want our pictures taken right now. We came here for privacy."

He chuckled. "Why not? You girls look great." He laughed off my comment and snapped a few pictures anyway. After taking close-up pictures of us, he slowly walked away.

Just a few days later, I sat on the team bus next to Erica, trying to get comfortable for a bus ride. She was sitting on the aisle seat with her feet up and her knees against her chest, wearing shorts. Less than five rows away, Mr. Russell sat with our head coach. Most of my teammates, including Erica, wore headphones listening to music. I wasn't wearing my headphones when I overheard Mr. Russell tell our head coach, "Man, look at those legs. Can you believe those legs? They are so toned."

I can't be the only one hearing this, I just can't be, I thought.

The head coach responded, "Hey, cool it man. She's just a kid!"

Mr. Russell didn't say anything more. My relief was mixed with a sudden disgust and fear because now he was showing interest in Erica, too. My basketball trip to Australia turned into something more sinister and scary for me. Not only did I have to look out for myself and deal with my warring emotions, I was feeling responsible for my younger friend.

After returning home from Australia, the car rides home from Mr. Russell's house continued. I never knew on any given ride if something was going to happen or not. He was unpredictable, and I never felt safe, especially since he threatened me not to tell. As my family and the Russell family grew closer, I found it more and more difficult to tell anyone.

CHAPTER 6

Jake and I started ninth grade at the same private school. We didn't have many of the same classes together, yet we did spend some of our time in a group, sharing our love of sports and culture. However, there was one time each day I could count on seeing him, where we could share a few laughs. Jackie had her own car, so each morning Stephanie and I car-pooled with Jackie and Jake to school.

Mr. Russell didn't like that Jake saw less of me. He periodically asked my parents questions about me—what I was up to, whom I was with, and if I was dating. My parents often commented upon Mr. Russell's seemingly strange questions. However, not being familiar with the grooming actions of child predators, his questions failed to arouse suspicion.

One overcast morning in January, during my ninth-grade year I decided to sleep in. That particular morning, I made myself a breakfast of French toast and eggs. Afterward, I got comfortable on the couch to watch weekend cartoons. Mom had somewhere to be and took Lauren. Stephanie had stayed with Jackie overnight, and Dad was on an errand. I had the whole house to myself.

I was still in my pajamas, sitting on the couch, when I heard the doorbell ring. Dad was "Mr. Safety" and told us to always look before opening the door. I followed his directions and looked through the peephole. It was Mr. Russell, *again,* featuring a dinner plate size smile and holding something in his hands. I assumed that my parents were expecting him over. *Maybe I didn't get the memo.*

I ignored his repeated knocks, while watching his phony smile disappear. "I'm dropping something off for your Dad," he said. "Your Dad knows I'm here."

He was talking through the door. *How did he know I was there? Dad will be back soon; he only went on a quick errand.* My pre-adolescent fourteen-year-old mind and optimism hoped for the best.

I finally cracked opened the door, just enough to stick my head out. He had on his big smile, again. "I talked to your Dad. I must have just missed him. He said that he might not be here, but to go ahead and drop this off." He gestured down with his eyes at the medium-sized box, pushed his shoulder against the door, and kept moving until he was in the middle of the dining room where he sat the package down on the table.

"So what are your plans today? I see you're still in your pajamas." His eyes lingered on my body.

I turned to go into the living room, thinking all the while he would take the hint and leave. He didn't. Instead, I heard soft footsteps right behind me. Without any warning, he reached for me.

Fear gripped my whole body. But I didn't want him to sense

how weak and helpless I felt. I stepped back, scowled, and said, "No!" I started for the front door, and that's when he finally got his hands on me.

He grabbed me around my waist and whispered in my ear, "Shh, Shh, Shh."

I grabbed his hands and tried with all my strength to pull them away. He cornered me up against the wall and held me so I couldn't move. It was no use. While I kicked and struggled, he removed one hand from my waist to lift my shirt and pull down my pants.

"Stop!" I yelled. "I don't like it!"

He forced his face against mine and whispered, "Yes, you do."

I never stopped trying to push him off.

Fighting back tears I said, "You have to go. I'm calling my Dad."

He looked at me with surprise and said, "Why? I'm just trying to help you. *We* aren't doing anything wrong." He threw his hands in the air and repeated himself, "I'm just trying to help you." As he walked out, he reiterated that he only came to drop off the package. He told me not to tell anyone about what "we" did or "I would be in big trouble."

His face turned angry red. I was afraid he could tear me apart, if he took a notion. "Don't you dare tell anyone about this or your life will be ruined. You want to stay at the private school and go to college don't you? You could ruin both our lives forever."

I closed and locked the door as soon as he stepped out. I was shaking, leaning against the door, totally exhausted, with only one thought: *This just can't be happening to me.*

I broke down into uncontrollable tears. Everything happened so fast. Yet, in my mind it played in slow motion. I could feel my heart beating. Suddenly, I found it hard to breathe. I leaned against the stairway and continued crying for several minutes. *I wasn't safe in my own home. How can I tell Dad that his own friend tricked him into being there? No one was there to see what happened. It's my word against his. He is a likeable family man and churchgoer. It doesn't add up. Who would believe this?*

This insidious thing was not supposed to happen to me. "No! No! No! This can't be," I screamed, with no one seeing or listening.

After Mr. Russell left, I paced up and down the stairs and took short walks, trying to figure out how I could face my parents again. *How could I possibly continue wearing the mask of a normal teenager at home and at school?*

I wondered how I would react when I saw Jackie and Jake next, and wondered how I would react when I saw Grace again. I didn't want to feel uncomfortable around Grace. I felt sorry for her. *Did she know what her husband really was?*

I felt a part of my spirit was no longer there and instead felt isolation and separation. Confused, I thought maybe God had abandoned me. It was difficult for me to pray that night. *Was I still good enough for God to love? Would God even hear my prayer now?* I didn't ask God for anything. Instead, I had questions. If He really loved me, how could He, the Almighty, let this happen?

I felt further from God than ever before. *Maybe I wasn't worthy enough for God to intervene?* Fear, loneliness, shame, and confusion filled my heart. I couldn't even bring myself to pray specifically about what happened. Yet, even with a shrinking faith, deep down, I felt that only God was the one who could truly help me. I gave into the overwhelming feelings of fear and shame and I wasn't brave enough to take the chance to tell. And

I concluded that since something like this was never mentioned at home, school, or church it must be something that was simply better left unspoken.

Mr. Russell seemed convinced that what he did was justified. *Did I do something to bring this on?* What happened in my own home weighed heavily on my mind. His razor-sharp words about ruining my life and everyone else's lives raced through my mind day and night. I didn't want to let anyone down or cause any social trauma for two families that would surely follow. Also, my mind wasn't settled that Dad wouldn't kill him before he could process any other options.

Our family continued to see the Russell family at least twice a week. At fourteen years old I felt I had two options. I could tell everyone about how he hurt me, or I could block it out. Recalling the occurrences was one horror, but sharing them out loud with Dad was another kind of horror. With each passing day I continued to minimize, minimize, and minimize. As long as it didn't happen again I thought I could handle myself.

As the winter months passed, I looked forward to one thing, our annual family spring-break vacation to Colorado. Mom is a Colorado native, and all her family resides there. I loved visiting Colorado and still do to this day. I just knew that this spring-break trip was going to be a blast, until one evening I heard Mom announce, "The Russells are coming to Colorado with us this year!" She added, "I've talked with your uncles, and they don't have a problem with them coming along."

I suddenly felt weak in my stomach, and it must have shown. Mom looked at me with a curious expression.

"What's the matter? Aren't you excited? This is a great opportunity for you and Jake to spend more time together."

I let out a deep sigh and said, "I would rather go without the Russells."

The morning we left for Colorado, we all chose our caravan cars. Just like the Florida trip we took two vehicles, a big van for each family. The two vans were packed with ski jackets, boots, and other thick winter apparel. Without hesitation, I urged Jake to ride with Mom, Grace, and me. The other option was to ride in the backseat with Dad and Mr. Russell. The idea of spending an entire week with Mr. Russell in Colorado made me sick to my stomach. Just like so many other things, I felt as though he ruined my "happy place" in Colorado.

During the ride, Jake and I watched movies, played games, and listened to music. We also packed our favorite junk food for the road. Jake snacked a lot and offered me the snacks he brought, but I didn't have the stomach to eat much of anything. Everyone seemed to be having a good trip. Well, everyone except for me.

I thought I was doing a good job of hiding my dissatisfaction, but it showed in other ways. I realized this during our first lunch stop at McDonalds. As we lined up to place our orders, Mr. Russell cut in line to be near me. The smell of his cologne overpowered me. The sight and smell of Mr. Russell, and the strong smell of cheese and hamburgers cooking on the grill made my stomach turn up-side-down.

Dad broke the line to ask me what I wanted to order. "Nothing, I'm not really hungry." I said.

He urged me to order something, even if I didn't feel well. As we waited for our food, Dad and Mr. Russell pushed tables and chairs together in the dining area so we could all sit at one table. After the chairs were arranged, Mr. Russell looked at me and pointed toward a chair next to where he intended to sit. I ignored him and sat down at the opposite end of the table. After everyone gathered their condiments they found their seats, and Mr. Russell offered (as he usually did) to say the blessing. I witnessed this event more times than I care to remember, but at this particular moment, a feeling of contempt for this person suddenly filled my whole body and soul like nothing had in the past. I kept my eyes closed for a short minute and said a little prayer of my own.

We arrived at Uncle Patrick's house early in the evening, tired and generally worn out from the twelve-hour drive. Uncle Patrick, a chiropractor with a Doctor of Chiropractic degree, was ready with his portable adjustment table to smooth our kinks. Before it was over, my other uncle, Donovan, who is also a chiropractor, showed up to lend a hand.

Breakfast the next morning was a loud family reunion. My Aunt Roberta prepared a huge buffet of pancakes, eggs, and bacon. Together, we enjoyed coffee and breakfast as we shared stories from the road trip. As usual, Mr. Russell played his "nice guy" persona, telling jokes, laughing loudly, and generally doing his best to influence my uncles and their families that he was a part of the family. Not able to take it anymore, I left the kitchen to visit with my cousins.

When the adults were finished eating and "catching up" with each other over breakfast, they planned a two-day side trip. My uncles and their families were not able to leave their daily work responsibilities to join the trip.

We packed up and scurried back into the vans for a two-hour trip to a rented cabin located in the town of Breckenridge, the most magical place on earth in my eyes. The town is cozy, charming, and touristy, with crisp mountain air. The natural beauty of the whole scene was so out-of-this-world beautiful.

After getting settled in our cabin, we quickly made plans to explore as much as possible during our short stay. It was agreed that dog sledding, snowmobiling, and skiing would fill our days, and an evening carriage ride would fill our nights.

The cabin had something I was especially excited about: a hot tub. In fact, everyone was eager to get in and enjoy it. A wooden deck that allowed a magnificent view of the beautiful, snow-covered Rocky Mountains surrounded the hot tub.

At first sight of this gorgeous setup, I wanted to put on my bikini and jump in, even for just a few minutes. My mood changed quite suddenly when I pictured a familiar old man gawking at my body.

The others in our group left the deck to explore the remaining parts of our cabin. I inhaled a deep breath of fresh mountain air and continued to be amazed at the beauty of God's creation. As I turned to walk back into the cabin, my enthusiasm for all of this quickly vanished. Mr. Russell was standing not two feet from me, grinning like a feral cat with a cornered mouse. I backed off a few steps and stared at him. I could feel my throat getting tight as I struggled to keep myself together. A minute or two passed, but it seemed much longer before either of us spoke. My thoughts raced, but I was too choked up to speak. Finally I barely croaked, "Why don't you leave me alone for good?"

He dropped his shoulders with a sigh. "I thought we both understood what this trip could mean for us." He stepped toward me. "There are so many ways for us to lose everyone and try out some things I've been telling you about."

"You're *out* of your mind. There is no *'We.'* You're the one who doesn't understand. It was Mom's idea to invite you in the first place. There's something else you don't understand, Russell. If you don't quit harassing me, I'm just going to blurt it all out at the dinner table. Everyone will know, and I'll only have to say it once. If Dad doesn't kill you on the spot, you'll go straight to jail." His face turned into something that resembled a crazed animal, the same crazed animal I had seen so many times when he coached basketball games.

Even though Dad was only a shout away, I was frightened. My chest felt tight and I just wanted to scream. This had to stop—now! I didn't scream. I was determined to finally make a stand. My fright went away. I felt light-headed, and at that moment I was at my wits end. I said, "You've already destroyed my life. You've had all the fun you're going to have at my expense, Russell."

We stood, not far apart. He still had that menacing look on his face. In the past I would have been frightened enough to run, or maybe call for help. For what seemed like a long time, he stared me down. Without saying a word, he turned to leave, then stopped and whirled around to face me again. With his brow raised he said, "OK, you do what you want, but this isn't over yet. You can't make me believe you're that stupid."

Part of what he said was right. I wasn't stupid, not to him, anyway. I didn't blurt out anything at the dinner table or at any other occasion to tell everyone, or even one person. He knew I wouldn't. He had probably practiced these same techniques many times before. When I came to realize all of this, I convinced myself I was either stupid or crazy, or simply trapped with no way out. I felt caught in a no-win scenario.

Everyone else but me seemed to enjoy the hot tub together that second night at the cabin. I first counted heads in the tub to be sure everyone was accounted for before walking back inside for a cup of hot cocoa. I knew I had to be quick. I jumped out of the hot tub as fast as I could, grabbed a towel, and headed for the cabin door.

Mr. Russell came out of nowhere to follow me. I didn't hear shuffling feet until he was near enough to touch me. I was pouring a cup of cocoa when I jumped while turning to face him. I held back a scream. "I had to take a restroom break," he suddenly whispered. In almost the same breath he muttered again, "You look so sexy in that swimsuit."

Struggling to keep my even temperament, I moved toward the door with my drink in hand. He didn't stop his vulgar talk until we were close enough to everyone that he could be heard. Walking back to the hot tub, I felt a new and unfamiliar emotion. For the first time, I felt upset with Grace. *How could she not know that her husband was a pervert—a self-centered, vulgar, conniving pervert?*

Regardless of my miserable interactions with Mr. Russell, I felt grateful for the opportunity to spend some time in a beautiful setting, and experience a few firsts on our last day in Breckenridge: my first sleigh ride, dog sledding, and dinner in an outdoor tent below the snowy Rocky Mountains.

Arriving back home in Texas, I felt threatened more than ever by Mr. Russell. The cohesive friendship glue that bonded my family with the Russells was getting stronger. I could not escape him. As time passed, he continued to find ways to invade my peace of mind and privacy in more ways and in more areas of my life.

CHAPTER 7

The following year, Mr. Russell volunteered to be one of the coaches for my tenth-grade spring basketball team. So, again, I was at his mercy, unable to get away from his one-track mind. I loved basketball, it was my safe place, and I was good at it. When I was on the gym floor, either practicing or playing a game, that was my whole world—it didn't at all resemble the fogged-up landscape that I viewed life through on a daily basis the past few years.

As a coach, Mr. Russell used intimidation to get his way. He was loud, aggressive, and ostensibly took too far what he called coaching. In fact, he was often thrown out of games because of his loud, verbal abuse directed toward the officiating referees.

During the spring basketball season we had practice twice a week. On our way home the second day of practice Dad glanced at me and said, "Mark Russell told me today it would be no extra trouble at all for him to bring you home after practice from now on since he drives right by our street on the way to the gym. Sometimes it's hard to adjust my schedule to pick you up on time. From now on neither of us will have to worry about me being late."

I slumped in the car seat and never said a word the rest of the way home, realizing I had experienced my last day of enjoyment from basketball practice. Instead of using my mind to learn the plays, I concentrated on how to fight off Coach Russell's free hand on the way home.

"Have you had sex with anyone yet?" he asked, on one of our first trips home together. "If you have, it's OK. You can tell me. I won't tell anyone." The thought entered my mind to open the door and jump out of the speeding car. "No, I am waiting," I said.

He went on and explained how "real sex" would feel. Everything was described in great detail. He also carried on about how the feelings were different for men and for women.

I was sitting slightly slumped, hands clasped between my knees, looking straight ahead.

Barely able to breathe, I said, "I don't want to talk about such things or I'm going to tell my parents."

He said, "What we talk about in private *better* be just between us, or you'll be responsible for ruining both of our lives."

How could I find the right words that would finally convince him that I wasn't interested in discussing sex or doing anything with him? In desperation, I said, "Why do you keep going on like this anyway, when I've made it perfectly clear to you so many times that I'm not now, or ever will be, interested in doing such things with you. It's just crazy to even think about."

My constant objections never stopped him from his neverending monologues on any of our rides home. Unless he asked me a direct question, I rarely said anything on the short ride from the gym to my home. But that didn't stop Mr. Russell from going on and on about how "our plans" to get together should be arranged, how he wanted to be a new kind of "coach" for me—a "Sex Coach."

I finally broke the silence. Looking straight at him while he drove, I shouted, "I don't need a sex coach. And as I've told you a thousand times, I don't want to hear anymore about sex from you."

He removed his hands momentarily from the steering wheel and raised both of them in front of him in a show of futility.

"Can't you understand I'm doing you a favor? You'll be grateful for the teachings when you finally do have sex with your future boyfriend or husband."

He parked the car in front of our house and immediately reached over and put his hand far up my leg. I pushed it away with my left hand, quickly opened the door with my right hand, and heaved my way out the door.

When I was clear of the car, I held the door open partway, leaned over, and spoke with as much conviction as I could muster, "When I get in the house I'm going to tell my parents everything."

It was almost dark out by then, but I could see well enough from the dome light that he had a scowl on his face and a crazed look in his eyes.

In a strained tone of voice, he muttered, "They won't believe a word you say, and you'll sit on the bench for the rest of the season."

I slammed the door and ran to the house.

I didn't believe for one minute that he would take my threat seriously—and he didn't. On our future trips he only became more determined to have me see his point of view. In so many twisted words, he did his best to make me feel as though I was willingly taking part in everything, despite the fact that I was verbally, and physically, fighting off all of his advances.

Days and weeks passed. But despite it all, I didn't willingly submit to any of his vile persuasiveness. In time, I started to believe that since I wasn't punching him in the face, or dialing 911, that *it was my fault. I must be a bad person. God must not love me. I am not worth protecting.* He threatened my life and my upcoming year of high school basketball. *He had already taken my dignity and stolen my innocence. What more could he do?*

Many times I thought (or maybe I dreamed it) that, some day, in a state of total anguish and disgust, and scared to the core, I would just blurt it all out, and watch everyone, from somewhere above. Some of my family (including me) may not even live through all of it to see the ending. It would simply be too much to bear. After imagining all of this at the time, of course, I couldn't possibly tell anyone. I felt caught in a no-win scenario.

I resented going to basketball practice and wanted the season to end as soon as possible. It started to show. I didn't play very well during games. Dad even suggested one-on-one skill-developing lessons, since I was noticeably underperforming. If anyone asked me about my performance, I was indifferent. My lack of passion showed before, during, and even after games.

My frustration and anger grew to a point that I started to rebel during practice and at games. If Mr. Russell yelled at me to hustle, I did the opposite. The only reason I didn't give it all up was because I couldn't think of a reason to explain my actions to my parents, and I didn't want to give up my athletic status with the school. Troubled and confused with all of these thoughts, I decided to finish the season.

On another ride home, Coach Russell must have decided to

get smart, maybe fearing that I was at a "tipping point" of saying something to my parents. For whatever reason, he stopped talking about his wishful sexual experiences with me, and went on to details about his early sex life with his wife, Grace, when they first became intimate.

I felt sorry for Grace. Her husband was a sick person, and I wished she could come to her own conclusion about it. He continued to tell me about years of their sex life together. Every time I interjected, he would interrupt me and reply, "It's good information to know."

As I was getting out of the car, Coach Russell said, "Oh, I slipped an early birthday present into your gym bag. Let me know what you think about it?"

Instead of responding, I shut the door and walked away.

When I was in my room, I unzipped my gym bag with curiosity, mixed with fright. *What has he done now?* I thought. I pulled out a newly bought toy from the adult store. I gasped. *What does he think he is doing sneaking this into my bag?* I felt shameful to even *touch* such a perverse object. I had to get rid of it as fast as I could.

I rushed downstairs and grabbed some grocery store bags from a kitchen cabinet, wrapped up the horrific thing, and took it straight to the big trash bin outside in the alleyway. As I stood, staring at the trash bin, I shook my head. *What a feeble, perverted attempt to get me comfortable with his suggestive sexual conversations.*

Finally, the spring basketball season was approaching its end. I was probably more excited than anyone else. The whole season was a big disappointment for me. It seemed like nothing else in the whole world mattered anymore except for ending the season. I could see a dim light at the end of the tunnel. It was not a very bright light—but I had to believe it was God's endeavor to renew my hope that I could, again, take control of my life.

CHAPTER 8

One morning, as I rolled out of bed and put my feet on the floor, my first thought was, *one more week of basketball season—God help me.* At that moment, I felt an unusually strong need for encouragement. Still not totally awake, I started searching my mind for a short Bible verse to start my day. During my prayer I recalled a verse I had to memorize for Bible class somewhere in the book of Matthew: *So have no fear of them, for nothing is covered that will not be revealed, or hidden that will not be known.* I can do that, I promised myself.

I was still holding out hope I could change the circumstances of my life if only I could escape the daily close-up encounters with Coach Russell. That didn't happen. All that happened in the past would seem like a picnic compared to what was to come.

On Saturday, a nonpractice day, Coach Russell called Dad to tell him our team's new basketball jerseys had arrived in the mail. He said they sent all the wrong sizes. He asked Dad to drop me off at his house to take a look at them. Dad told me Mr. Russell wanted to know right away because they could be reordered. Dad explained all this to me, with none of it making any sense. We didn't need new uniforms, and even if we did, they wouldn't be used until the fall school term. Dad hurried me out of the house and dropped me off at Mr. Russell's home. He asked me to call him when I was done checking out the jerseys. "It shouldn't take you long," he said.

Coach Russell offered a friendly wave to Dad. Then he walked me inside. He was the first to speak, confessing that he hadn't checked all the jerseys, but the ones he'd checked were all the same sizes. "You can help me check all of them before we let the other girls try them on," he said. "Anyway," he went on, "I want to see how they look on you first."

As he turned about to face me, he said, "So, I've been meaning to ask you how you enjoyed the special gift I got you? It was one of the best ones they had."

I was nervous and hyper-aware now. "You must be crazy. I threw the horrible thing away."

"You WHAT? You didn't even try it? That's rude, when I went out of my way to buy it for you."

I slowly backed away from him. "You're lucky," I said. "In some countries they cut off your hands and feet for owning a filthy thing like that. My Dad would do a lot more than just cut off your hands and feet." I didn't know for sure about my statement on the actions of other countries, but it sounded good. I knew positively sure what Dad would do to Mr. Russell.

I walked to the window and lifted the blinds. By now I had figured out that Grace and the kids weren't there, and I didn't know when they were expected back. But I wanted him to think about the possibility. Something was so terribly wrong here, and I was too rattled to think of a way out. I turned away from the window, almost touching Mr. Russell's outstretched hand, still holding the jersey.

I grabbed the jersey out of his hand and walked to the guest bathroom, and locked the door, which allowed me a brief sense of security.

The jersey was a perfect fit. Even though I was suspicious from the beginning, it was a terrifying moment. I was in deep trouble. He would stop me if I ran for the door, and I didn't know if anyone was expected back soon. My phone was on the kitchen counter where I left it last, but it may as well have been thirty miles away.

Sitting on the cool, tile bathroom floor with a tangle of emotions racing through my mind and body, the full weight of the situation was overpowering. I was frightened out of my mind, and feeling, really, really stupid and embarrassed. *From everything I had been through so far, how could I have ever allowed him to pull a rotten thing like this on me?*

I was fifteen years old, trapped in a bathroom, and fearing for my safety in a serious way. The bathroom was small, and getting smaller by the minute. I could almost feel the walls closing in on me.

As near as I could judge time, about ten minutes had lapsed, and I was still sitting on the bathroom floor, with my knees pulled up to my chest, both hands holding my face. It seemed like a long time because I had few options to consider, and I knew Coach Russell was impatient to get on with whatever was on his mind. My only hope was that Dad, or someone else would return unexpectedly and foul his plans.

Then I heard a knock on the bathroom door. His knocks were soft and easy at first. When I didn't answer the knock, he tried again, much louder this time. I heard him say, "Did the jersey fit? I need to see if you have a good fit." I had already changed back into my everyday clothes and couldn't swallow the lump in my throat. I was trapped.

I turned the lock on the door and opened it a few inches to see him standing about two feet away. He pushed the door open some more and stood staring at me for what seemed a long time, his eyes searching my entire body. "I thought you were going to show me how you looked in it?" He said, in a little boy tone of voice.

Without saying a word, or looking directly at him, I started toward the kitchen to get my phone. I stopped as he stepped in front of me. To break the silence I said, "I don't see a problem with the jersey. It fit me perfectly."

He caught my arm and turned me toward him as I moved to step around him. "I have a movie I want you to see," he said. He moved to the kitchen counter to grab two glasses of wine he had poured while I was changing and pushed my phone aside. Holding one glass up toward me, as for a toast, he said, "Let's have some wine and relax for awhile."

"No!" I shook my head.

"Well, it's here if you change your mind," he said, as he casually placed the glass of wine back on the counter.

It was all coming back to me now, from past encounters with him. He knew all the right moves and words to say until the time was just right, and then it would be too late for me. Then he grabbed the TV remote and pressed the play button as he moved to the side to give me a full view. I glanced at the screen, and then quickly turned my head away. I knew what was coming. "Have you ever seen one of these movies?" he asked. "It's pornography," he added.

I looked toward the closed door and didn't immediately respond. He asked the question again. "No," I answered. "But I know what it is. Please turn it off."

He didn't move.

Grabbing my phone off the kitchen counter, I walked to the opposite side of the living room and dialed. He bolted across the room and yanked the phone out of my hand.

Then he grabbed me around my waist with both hands. He leaned in to kiss me, and I pushed him away as hard as I could. But it was no use. He was just too strong. After being forced to the couch, I was in survival mode, fighting too hard to be aware of how much danger I was facing. The harder I fought the more restless and violent he became. All the while I was fighting him off, he was shouting, "No, no."

He unzipped his pants and fully exposed himself. By then I knew I was completely trapped, and defenseless, unless someone came to save me. *During all that time my thoughts were focused on how to escape. If I could just get loose of his grip—maybe I could run to the neighbors, down the street—anywhere.*

As he continued to advance, I did my best to fight him off. He was so strong and heavy I could barely breathe under his force. But I kept fighting, even when I could feel my heart beating out of my chest in sheer exhaustion and panic.

"Shh!" He repeated over and over. "I'm doing you a favor, you will thank me later. I'm your coach remember."

I kept saying, "No, no," with all the breath I had left. But, it didn't stop him from having his way with me until something interrupted him.

My cell phone rang and I tried to jump up and answer it. Coach Russell scolded, "It can wait, unless it's your father." He stopped, picked up the phone, and looked at the caller before saying, "It's your father. You better let him know you're *OK*." For the first time ever, I sensed real fear in Coach Russell's tone of voice.

I was choking with a big lump in my throat and fighting

back tears. I gathered myself the best I could, and Coach Russell handed me the phone. Almost in a shout I said, "Hi, Dad," as loudly as I could with the state of my throat, leaving no doubt in Coach Russell's mind *who* was on the phone.

I turned away and looked out the window, knowing he was scrambling to get his clothes back on. "He's right around the corner," I stated.

After I straightened myself up, Coach Russell started talking again. "What did you think of that? Didn't that feel good?" With that he added, "I can teach you lots of ways to feel good."

In my state of mind, I had nothing to say. With Dad just around the corner, I felt almost safe. I simply glared at him with intense hatred, walked through the door, and waited outside for Dad to arrive.

He followed me outside and stood so close behind that I could actually feel my skin crawl. "This is our secret," he ranted, "if you tell, your life is over."

Dad pulled into the street and parked in front of the house. I didn't wait for him to park or get out of the car before I approached him. I was distraught, but I knew I had to be careful. I walked to the car as if I had not just experienced the worst thirty minutes of my entire life.

Coach Russell casually stepped around the car to the driver side, and Dad rolled his window down. Then Coach Russell confidently placed his hands on the ledge of the driver's window. Using the window ledge to support his elbows, he leaned forward to talk with Dad. He greeted Dad with a relaxed smile, saying, "We checked all the jerseys and they seem to be just fine. We shouldn't have to reorder anything. Thanks for dropping her by." Before Dad could even reply, he continued, "Hey, how about a movie tonight, Greg?"

CHAPTER 9

That night, Dad went to a movie with Coach Russell. After the movie, Dad called to ask if I had eaten dinner. After what seemed like a long pause, wondering if I could ever face my own father again, I stuttered, "Yeah, yeah, dinner would be good." I was so emotional I couldn't remember if I had eaten anything all day. After consenting to the meal out, I started to have anxious reservations. I felt tired all over and was suffering from a weak stomach. I seriously questioned if I could get my act together enough to sit across the table from my Dad without bursting into tears.

Dad opened the door to the restaurant and I walked in ahead of him, almost into the outstretched arms of Mr. Russell, standing in the foyer, showing a knowing grin. Dad didn't mention Mr. Russell was joining us for dinner. Abruptly, I turned and stared at Dad, with what I thought was an unbelieving look. When I turned back, Mr. Russell's happy face had vanished, to be replaced by a look of irritation and disappointment. He scowled at me, and I didn't miss what I thought looked like a warning in his demeanor.

Before we were even seated, I asked to be excused and walked toward the ladies' room, hoping that I could get in there and calm my clenched stomach before embarrassing myself. Standing over the toilet, staring at the wall, I inhaled deep breaths in hopes of regaining my composure. But no matter how hard I tried, the tears still came, with noises like a sick child. I hunched over and started to get nauseous with dry heaves. My stomach was empty.

In my struggle to throw up, I noticed a bump on my wrist. I had felt it itch, but I hadn't noticed the visible red welt. The tears were still coming as I kept finding itchy red spots on my upper body. I was so shook up. *How could I go back to the table and even begin to act normal enough to sit through a meal?*

When I finally recovered enough to leave the restroom and return to the table, I told Dad that I wasn't feeling well. I showed him my wrist and whimpered, "Look, it's like a rash or something."

Dad was never much for showing outward emotions. And when he did, it was time to sit up and pay attention. After examining the rashes on my arms and legs for what seemed like several minutes, he turned to me with an anxious expression. "I don't like the looks of this. Do you know if something bit you? Does it hurt?"

"It's not a bug bite, Dad. I think it's some kind of rash."

"How could it be a rash? You've never been allergic to anything."

Enough of all of this, I thought, *I just want to go home.* I, again, made my desires clear to Dad, and he promptly slid out of his seat, leaving Mr. Russell with a disappointed look. Mom wanted to know all about our evening, but Dad and I interrupted her questioning and told her about my rash. I lifted up my pants to my knee to show her. "It feels like my skin is burning."

"Oh, Honey, I think you have hives!" she said. They both

agreed they needed to take me to the emergency room. I was getting worse by the minute.

After three hours in the emergency room, being poked and prodded by three different medical professionals, as a body, they concluded my hives were caused by stress. I wanted to tell, but my fear was stronger than my ability to overcome the shame. For I felt shameful to even speak of the things that Mr. Russell did to me in secret. And if I did tell, the threats would follow. We left the clinic with a prescription for ointment to control the burning, and an oral prescription to decrease itching—both bearing names I couldn't pronounce.

Settled into bed that night, I couldn't turn off my mind. *How had things turned so sour in my life?* Friends were avoiding me in hallways and other places, turning their heads or just staring straight ahead. There was a real chasm between my classmates and me. I had become accustomed to accepting rejection from my friends and casual acquaintances—I didn't blame them. But, the loneliness of shutting my sisters and parents out of my life was unbearable.

I was convinced God had totally abandoned me, and I was too ashamed to ask for any special treatment from Him. I started to believe that it was *because of me* that all of this was happening. After all, there must be something very wrong with me. I must be at fault, a bad person. If I did ask God for help He might bring to my attention something from the book of James, like, *Dear sister, when troubles come your way, consider it an opportunity for great joy,* or some other verse that didn't make any sense at a time when my skin was on fire with a rash, and my mind was wrestling with shame, doubt, anger, and self-hatred. *What was the use of trying to explain anything to Him, anyway? He was all knowing and could see right through me.*

Grace came to our house to inspect my hives (but not with the same interest as most of the other curious seekers who wanted to take a look). These are the same people you see slowing traffic on major highways to stare at an overturned car, with two ambulances and a fire truck in attendance.

Grace was different. She was a real, caring friend, and I welcomed her concern and offer of prayers. "You are just like one of my daughters," she said. *Wasn't that what her husband said to me? How could she not know?* Mom called Grace when my hives disappeared in a few days, giving credit to prayers and the several prescriptions and ointments prescribed by the physicians.

Gradually, internalizing all of this conflict and pain started to affect me in more serious ways, some of which I wasn't immediately aware. Aside from the obvious physical symptoms, it impacted my schoolwork, and I became socially withdrawn until I gradually ceased to be me.

My wounded heart had become hardened. To protect my heart from ever being hurt again, I emotionally isolated myself. I pushed God and everyone else onto the back burner of my life. And I even hid from myself. My life, empty of meaning, was a tangled mess of guilt, shame, blame, and fear.

It wasn't long after the hives disappeared that I started to lose my hair. I had gained weight intentionally and didn't bother to shower often; beauty was my enemy. I hoped that if I wasn't attractive, Mr. Russell would stop.

These changes were accompanied by my low energy level and general apathy toward life. It didn't go unnoticed by my parents. They made doctor appointments, again. This time I was tested for anemia and whatever could be found from the thyroid. The test results were all negative. And, it didn't end there—they were determined to find out what was wrong with me, but, despite the efforts of some of the best doctors in the Dallas Metro, there wasn't a single diagnosis offered, except for stress.

My grades plummeted steadily from mostly A's to C's, and I was failing math. I attended class regularly, seemingly paid attention, and mostly turned my assignments in on time. My classmates often joked about it and called me a "Zoner" because I was zoned out through most of my classes. I didn't care about school anymore, and my childhood dream of attending college was long forgotten.

While I appreciated my parents' efforts to help me, a part of me felt angry with them for not seeing Mr. Russell for who he *really* was. I can still remember, with regret, that I showed this anger toward them when they gave their real affection for me through hugging and whispers of reassurance. "Your hugs are limp," Mom complained. Dad never said a word about my lack of affection.

I reasoned they just didn't understand and forgave them on the spot. I couldn't love anyone or anything around me, and I didn't feel worthy of accepting love from them or anyone else. And it wasn't much relief fully realizing, deep down, it wasn't their fault. They did the best they could with the information they had—they knew nothing about the grooming actions of child predators, or the behavioral symptoms of a victimized child.

One day Jake invited me to shoot some hoops with him at the gym. He was worried about me, he confessed. We shot a round, laughed, and talked about our classes. Just when we were starting to enjoy our basketball socializing, Coach Russell made an unexpected appearance. Jake went to the restroom, and then it was just Coach Russell and me in the gym, alone.

I handled the basketball, ducked my head, and dribbled toward the corner of the gym. I felt his creepy presence behind me first, then the smell of his strong cologne, before he overtook me with long strides about halfway across the gym. "Hey, wait up," I heard him say.

I countered by dribbling the basketball toward the sidelines.

My efforts to avoid him proved futile. He grabbed the ball and slid over against me. After glancing in the direction Jake had gone and seeing no one, he said, in hushed tones, "I think about you and the other day all the time." Then, he said something into my ear so vulgar that I couldn't believe my ears.

Blood rushed to my brain and I almost slumped to my knees. *How dare he interrupt our basketball time with such filth?* I was so shaken, I can barely remember my response (if I even offered one).

But, whatever I said didn't dull his enthusiasm for ruining my day. He wanted to "tell me something," he said. "Remember me telling you that I had jury duty? Well, I didn't tell you the rest of it."

"I don't remember, and I don't want to hear about it." I turned my head and looked toward the restroom area where Jake had disappeared.

"Well, listen," he was whispering now. "This is something you need to think about. It was a case where a girl had been sexually abused." He cleared his throat, and I could feel my chest tighten. "Well, most of these kids aren't believed, anyway, so, as a jury we decided she was just making the whole story up. That happens so often, you know."

With a heavy heart, I felt my eyes tear up. He continued his monologue, explaining other details of the trial. "Now you know that if you ever tell anyone about us, it could ruin your life and mine. This is our secret and just like that little girl, no one will believe you. You realize how serious this is? Sometimes you scare the hell out of me, because you could ruin the lives of both our families for nothing. If I ever suspect you will tell, then . . ." Before he could finish his threat Jake started walking back toward us. He finished by saying, "I know I can trust you not to say anything."

When Jake came back, I asked him to take me home. *How much more could I take?* I desperately needed to make sense of what was happening. I thought about how close I was to both my sisters. They seemed safe from Mr. Russell. Jackie also seemed comfortable around her father. *Was I the only one?*

While agonizing, trying to make sense of it all, I started feeling something familiar on my skin. My whole body itched. *Oh no, not again!* I waited, hoping the itching would stop. It didn't. My small rashes had turned into hives that spread over most of my body. My whole body felt as though it was on fire. My anger at my inability to control my sense of security continued to build as I worked harder to suppress the trauma and rage.

So, I tried to focus on something that would make me happy. My birthday was only a few days away. Birthdays were always a big celebration at our house. Maybe turning sixteen was just what I needed, and I desperately wished for a car.

I made it clear to my parents how important a car was to me, without giving away anything. They asked me questions about the type of party I wanted, *if I* were to have a party. I explained, again, I didn't *want* a party. I just wanted a car so I could *choose* where I went. The car was my magic carpet for keeping Mr. Russell far away. He would never drive me anywhere again. I needed that car to believe that he would never dominate me again—ever.

This would be a birthday I would never forget.

CHAPTER 10

On Sunday, April 6, my sixteenth birthday, we had just arrived home after church and a long lunch. I still hadn't changed out of my church clothes when I heard the doorbell. I was closest, so I peeked through the blinds, and then opened the door to greet Jake Russell. He was wearing a cute little smile, and his face was lit up with anticipation—of what I couldn't guess.

After being welcomed by my family he turned back to me. "Happy birthday," he said without losing his smile. "Do you want to take a little drive with me—go somewhere fun for your birthday?"

"That sounds great," I exclaimed, without even thinking about it. Jake had received a car for his birthday sometime before school started last fall, and he occasionally stopped by for a trip to Starbucks, or another favorite place of mine. We saw less of each other my sophomore year, so it was nice to spend some time with him.

As we left the driveway, he said, "If you don't mind, Mom and Dad made me promise to bring you by the house. They probably have a little gift for you, or something."

I gulped. "Sure, but only for a little bit," I said. I was uneasy. *Too much had happened in that house.*

When I walked through the door, I heard a chorus of loud voices scream, "SURPRISE!" I looked into the living room and saw most of my classmates standing and clapping; the same classmates I felt distanced from for so long. There were birthday decorations, balloons, and familiar faces smiling. And party music played in the background. On the verge of tearing up, I wandered through the house, talking over the music, greeting and thanking everyone. There was a carefully decorated table display in the kitchen with a custom cake. Also on the table was a white T-shirt with a large number 16 printed on it. It was filled with colorful, handwritten signatures and personal messages from the guests.

My friends at school hadn't abandoned me after all. My heart was full from all the positive attention. Lately it seemed that I was only getting attention I didn't want. Mom and Dad made sure that my favorite foods were prepared. I could smell them cooking. Everyone seemed to have a good time, smiling and laughing. I had almost, just almost, forgotten that I was standing in the enemy's den, and I didn't overlook the simple fact that I needed to keep a sharp eye out for the unknown. He could appear any moment and spoil my birthday. Fifteen minutes or so had passed before I actually started to feel safe with all the familiar faces milling around me.

Grace was standing near the cake table with Mom and Dad. I walked to the table, gave them hugs, and thanked them for arranging such a terrific surprise party. Then that awful cologne smell that brought so much terror into my life hit me like an avalanche of stones. I froze. I couldn't move my eyes away from him. There he was, grinning with what looked like pride. No matter what, I thought, I wasn't going near this awful person. But he had other plans.

He walked right into me with outstretched arms. I had no place to go without making a fuss. He squeezed me hard and whispered into my ear, "Happy Birthday, Baby." Releasing me from his grip, but still holding me apart with hands on my shoulders, he showed me his winning smile. I so wanted to scream and slam a frying pan right into his face.

Despite what just happened, I decided to keep calm and focus on the other people who had given so much thought and energy to make the occasion special for me. I was surprised to see so many people there. Fellow students surrounded me along with my family. The party lasted for most of the day and into part of the evening.

After cake and presents, guests started to leave. When everyone left, I was able to read some of the messages they wrote on my T-shirt. I had turned into a hermit over the last two years, but the comments reassured me that people still cared and that I was not invisible. For the first time in a long time, I felt noticed and appreciated by my fellow classmates.

While reading the messages, I came across Mr. Russell's—it was repulsive. No one else who read the inscription on the shirt could possibly know what his comment meant. My palms started to sweat, and I thought that maybe my heart would stop. When I felt my face getting red, I rushed to the bathroom before having to face anyone straight on. His obscene thoughts, written by his own filthy hands were now inscribed, forever, on my memorable birthday T-shirt. Most of my joy from the surprise party was lost the moment I read his message. The words "*Sweet* 16" no longer had the same meaning.

The car I hoped for wasn't at my birthday party. Afterward, my parents told me that they were planning on buying me a car, but the final arrangements hadn't been completed. I was disappointed, of course, but I knew my parents would be true to their word.

Since Mr. Russell threatened me if I told, I knew I had to keep silent. This was especially true after they had opened their home and went through so much work to make my day special. I knew I couldn't cope with my silence much longer. But, this wasn't the time. Shackled with shame and burdened with bitterness toward my current life situation, I felt out of options to cope with the mass of my inner pain. Crying was not soothing anymore.

I took a safety pin from inside my backpack and sat on the edge of my bed. I took a deep breath, pulled up my pant leg, and cut myself for the first time. I thought about cutting my wrists, but realized the cuts would be too easily visible to others. It hurt a lot worse than I thought it would. But I felt emotional pain leaving my body. At last I had tried something with an external physical match to my internal emotional turmoil. It was cathartic. At the time, this drastic action worked. I could express my anger turned inward. Finally, I had control over the cause of my pain.

Five months later, in September, Dad took me to look at cars. This was the moment I had been waiting for. I didn't care what kind of vehicle I got, as long as I had something dependable. Dad wanted me to pick out some specific models he thought I would like. We visited car dealerships, and I test-drove more cars than I could count. There were so many cars that I liked. My thoughts raced, and I just couldn't make up my mind.

Finally, I looked at Dad and said, "Let's just buy them all, and I'll make up my mind later."

Dad looked at me with a straight face and said, "OK, since it's your birthday." We had a good laugh and continued our search. We eventually test-drove a car that I did love, immensely. Dad suggested that I ". . . sleep on it," since I had changed my mind so often. The next day I let Dad know I really wanted the car. I didn't want to press him, but Homecoming school activities were just days away.

Although Homecoming was right around the corner I had not been asked for a date yet. But I can't say that I was surprised, just disappointed. My hair was still falling out, and I had intentionally gained a lot of weight to make myself unattractive for Mr. Russell or other males who might want to get physical.

Homecoming Court nominees were announced over the school intercom on the Monday before the big night. I was only half listening when I heard "Jenna Quinn" announced. I couldn't believe it—my third year to be nominated. It didn't seem real, owning to what was so obvious to everyone: my personality, social life, physique, school grades, and extracurricular activities were all in the dumps.

On Friday night of the Homecoming game I could sense there was something going on with my parents—a family secret, maybe—something that was rarely kept in my family. They asked over and over, "Are you excited for the game?"

With my current nomination I was anxious to get to the stadium. Dad had left the house to ". . . get something," he announced, and Mom and my sisters were still dressing. When Dad returned to the house, he leaned over and whispered something in Mom's ear. Mom turned, looked toward me, and said, "Jenna, your dad wants you to go outside and help him carry in some things."

"But, Dad, we're going to be late for the game," I reasoned.

"That's OK. This will only take a minute."

When I saw what was parked in front of the house, I put my hands in front of my face and cried out, "Oh! My gosh! I can't believe this!"

Dad repeatedly asked, "What do you think?"

I could barely speak. With my hands still covering my face, I said, "I love it. It's the car I wanted."

The car was for real, and it belonged to *me*. I literally jumped into the driver's seat. With my hands on the steering wheel, I leaned back to soak in the feeling. I turned the music on, looked in the back seat, checked the compartments, and played with the dashboard buttons. My ray of hope came in the form of an old 1997 Infinity J30.

On the Saturday following Homecoming weekend, I was relaxing in my bedroom when my cell phone rang. I didn't recognize the number because I wasn't quick to add contacts in my phone.

As an eager sixteen-year-old, I pushed the button and said, "Hello." The first words I heard were: "Hi, Jenna. This is Mark Russell," and he just kept on talking.

"You must be really excited about your new car. How do you

like it? I couldn't wait to talk to you after I found out you were getting one."

When I heard Mr. Russell's voice on the line, my heart sank. Horror gripped me. I held the phone without saying anything for what seemed a long time. It probably wasn't more than five seconds, but thoughts raced through my mind about how to best handle this. *Would he stop calling me if I just pushed the off button when his number appeared? Should I really unload on him in my reply?* Before I could decide what my reaction should be, he started up again.

"I think of you all the time." He continued, "I can't wait to see you again."

My blood boiled with frustration.

I pushed the off button and threw myself flat on the bed. I could almost feel my skin crawling. I turned on my side and stared at the walls, imagining him watching me at this instant through binoculars.

At that moment, it was clear to me that Mr. Russell was not backing down. *What was I going to do now?*

CHAPTER 11

During the fall of my junior year my physical appearance continued to change to a sight that was blaringly apparent to me and to those closest to me. It showed that physical attractiveness was the last thing I cared about. I wore big black wristbands, dog-chain chokers, and dark-colored T-shirts when I wasn't in school uniform. I showered maybe once every three days and gained an extra twenty pounds. Even with my plaid uniform skirt, I wore a thick dark hooded sweatshirt over my oxford button up. I simply withdrew because I didn't feel safe to connect with anyone, in even the safest of situations.

It was a busy time for everyone in the family that year. It was Stephanie's first year in college, and Lauren was in seventh grade. We girls kept my parents incredibly busy. But even with our busy schedules, Mom and Dad let me know they were aware and worried about my changed looks and behavior. I knew all along they were worried sick about me because they tried to trap me at every opportunity to discuss what was obviously, to them, a serious problem. One or both of them together would look me straight in the eyes and start out with something like: "Honey, we are so worried about you. Is there anything at all we can do to help? You know that you can tell us anything, anything at all."

I knew they meant well, of course, but I wasn't even put together enough myself to be bothered about their state of mind. On these occasions, which I gradually learned to anticipate, I would quickly retreat to my room and usually stay there until one or the other of my parents knocked, then the familiar, "Honey, are you all right?"

My response was practiced: Put down my Bible, or wipe the tears from my cheeks, clear my throat, then reply, in a cheerful voice: "Sure, I'm OK. Just doing some schoolwork." Or maybe I would say, "Just reading my Bible." All of this became a learned response and could have just as easily been a bold-faced lie as the truth. And none of this concerned me, either. At this point I wasn't living in the real world and didn't attach much importance to my words or actions, anyway. My heart was still hardened. I continued to emotionally isolate myself to keep myself from being hurt again.

When basketball season started at school the fall of my junior year I wasn't exactly thrilled. Right off, the school coaches noticed my total disregard for the game. I didn't care much because my mind wasn't with the world of sports anymore. Physically, I went through the motions at practice and during games. This was the first time since I picked up a basketball that I was relegated to the bench, where I sat out most of the games. Aside from my school and Bible studies, basketball had always been foremost on my mind. It was a major part of my identity with the school, my friends, and my self-esteem. I understood perfectly well all of these changes in my life, but I felt powerless to do anything to change it. My energy, hopes, and dreams were zapped.

When Mom told me I was beautiful one day, it set me on a course to say something. I truly felt I was ugly, inside and out. Somehow I needed to show her how I felt because over time she wasn't really buying my learned responses. I didn't know if I was brave enough to do it all at once, but I owed my parents something. And it was painfully clear I had to stop evading their questions—their sanity and mine was at stake. I would tell Mom about cutting myself—today. *Maybe that would lead to something?*

I asked Mom to follow me to my room. As we walked together up the stairs, I said, "I have something to show you."

Mom quietly closed the door behind us and walked to the center of the room, where she stopped to face me. After allowing myself some deep breaths, trying to reassure myself, I started: "Mom, I have to show you something." Slowly, I bent over and lifted up my pant leg to my ankle where I had recently cut myself.

Some of the cuts were deeper than others, but they were all easily visible to the naked eye. She was on her knees, her face very close to my leg, making it impossible for me to see her face straight on, but I could hear her saying, over and over, "Oh, Honey," as she ran her fingers over each scar.

Mom finally rose to a standing position and stood very composed. I could see the sadness and exasperation on her face when she finally found her voice. In a quiet tone, she said, "Jenna, why did you do this to yourself? How long has this been going on?"

I turned away and stood beside the bed. "It just makes me feel better, but it hasn't been going on that long."

Then I sat down on the bed, my feet dangling in space, squeezed my hands tightly between my knees, and looked straight at the wall ahead of me, over and over pleading to myself, *Don't say any more. My poor parents have suffered enough with-*

out me causing more disruption to their lives—and to the innocent people in both families. I could see plainly enough through the anguish and frustration on her face that she was nearly at the breaking point. That was the end of my hope of telling her the rest of the story. Somehow I had to protect them from any more heartache. There had even been moments when I felt like a martyr—a hero for keeping quiet—protecting everyone. Maybe this was one of those moments.

She pleaded with me to stop what I was doing. I didn't promise her I would stop—quite honestly I didn't know that I could—but I told her that I would try my best. She talked to me about other ways to relieve stress, offered to buy me a gym membership and pay for massages. She expressed her thanks, over and over, and her complete relief that I had confided in her.

She held me while rubbing her hands over my back, without a word of censure, or condemnation. While she held me, I felt her love so strongly that I was at the brink of blurting the whole thing out right there.

Stephanie was scheduled to come home for Thanksgiving break. I hadn't seen her since Homecoming festivities at my school, and I was so fired up about seeing her again. I was looking forward to watching our old favorite movies, playing board games, shopping, and all the other silly things we laughed so hard about.

One of our favorite pastimes at home was racing each other up the stairs, always screaming, "The last one up is a rotten egg." We were watching TV that first evening Stephanie arrived home from college when she up and challenged me to the race. She leaned in close to catch me as I ran ahead of her. Jokingly, she grabbed my ankle, shouting, "I'm gonna *get* you." Without thinking about my reaction, I turned to her and gave her a spiteful look. I yelled back and slapped her hand from grabbing me. "That's not a funny joke!" I stormed upstairs into my room and slammed the door.

That was the first time I ever yelled at her with resentment in my voice. She couldn't know what her comment meant to me. I knew deep down my sister would never hurt me. She knocked on the door and asked me to come out. "Just leave me alone please," I responded. I would later learn how this incident would change my life forever.

As the cold weeks passed Stephanie came back home again for Christmas break. All three sisters were together again and carried out our favorite traditions. One of our Christmas traditions was baking. Mom, Stephanie, Lauren, and I watched Christmas movies as we baked together. We made peanut butter blossoms, rice crispy wreaths, chocolate fudge, and sugar cookies. As far back as I can remember, I have memories of us in the kitchen baking together.

Every year Mom always took the opportunity to teach us proper "cooking etiquette." Year after year she tried to teach us the same cooking methods over and over and over again. We knew how particular she was about closely following directions and, as sisters, our tradition was to mess them up. We loved to get a reaction out of her. With all the seriousness I could muster, I said, "So Mom, I put five cups of salt in the batter right?" Slowly, I tilted the measuring cup filled with salt over the mixing bowl. Mom gasped! We giggled. She didn't think the goofy questions were funny. She wanted us to pass the recipes on to the next generation. We also found humor in molding funny shapes with the batter.

One evening, during that Christmas break, the Russell family was invited to our home for a turkey dinner. I complained, "Why can't we enjoy the holiday with just our family?" Mom explained that she already invited them, and she couldn't un-invite them.

When the doorbell rang, Mom rushed to the door to greet our dinner guests. I backed off and stood behind Dad and my sisters. After the hugs and good cheer screams subsided, all the Russell family came trailing through the foyer, exchanging hugs and greetings with the girls and Dad. After greeting Jake and Jackie, I stepped back and started for the kitchen. It was a hopeless move, and I knew it at the time. Mr. Russell instantly moved his bowlegs ahead of me and quickly came forward with outstretched arms, pulled me to him, and held me until I was out of breath.

At the dinner table that evening, I was forced to watch this person, who made my life a living hell for the past few years, enjoy another meal at our family table. Self-assured, he spoke at the table, laughing and telling stories as if it were his own home, gushing with compliments about the food and making suggestions on how we could all spend the rest of the evening. I hurried to finish my meal, excused myself from the table, and informed everyone I was going to a friend's house.

After I left the dinner party, Mom informed me that Mr. Russell asked about me and seemed very concerned about my state of mind and physical condition, commenting that he noticed I had been gaining weight. He also seemed to be bothered by the fact that I had left the house. This all probably seemed very natural to everybody—except me.

Traditionally, Christmas Eve was just as much of a celebration as Christmas day. Mom threw a big Christmas Eve party at the house. She invited my aunts, uncles, cousins, friends, and, of course, the Russells. It would have been a perfect night, except for one person. Mr. Russell casually joked around with all my family members as he always did. He was like family to everyone. He was so comfortable, he even felt the need to bless the food before we ate. I didn't know how much more I could take of him in my home, laughing and carrying on.

After the party, I slept with Stephanie in her bed. It was a Christmas Eve tradition. We talked about how excited we were for Christmas. I tried to bribe her into telling me what she got me by telling her what her presents were. We helped Mom wrap presents that weren't our own, which meant we knew what the other sisters were getting. I was never good at keeping Christmas presents a secret. She laughed and said, "Not this year."

We said our goodnights and turned off the light. As I lay in bed, I could not help but wonder if Mom and Dad had made plans to see the Russells Christmas Day. In the past, we usually went over to their home Christmas Day for dinner. As I thought of yet another holiday ruined by Mr. Russell, I prayed for some sort of miracle.

CHAPTER 12

Mom was up early Christmas morning. She made a large breakfast of homemade cinnamon rolls, quiche, eggs, and pancakes. For her, the presentation was the key. We had to wait upstairs while she arranged the breakfast and gifts in just the right places. Sometimes we waited for thirty minutes before we were allowed downstairs. We knew better than to fuss about the time. A half-hour, or even an hour meant nothing to Mom. She had to get everything just perfect. The wait just added to the thrill of anticipation.

As a college student, Stephanie was used to sleeping in. No way was I going to allow that to happen on Christmas morning. I shook her. "Stephanie, wake up! It's Christmas morning!" I urged. Finally, and I mean *finally,* she wormed her way out of bed and made herself ready for the day we looked forward to all year. "Mom, are you ready?" I called downstairs. No response.

It was another fifteen or twenty minutes before we heard Mom call from the bottom of the stairs, "It's all ready. Come on down."

Right away I noticed that all the presents under the tree

were wrapped. On past Christmases, Mom left certain gifts unwrapped near our stockings. But before opening gifts, we ate breakfast first. I ate it as fast as I could. When everyone was finished eating, we all rushed to open our stockings.

Mom was standing behind me when she tapped me on the shoulder and asked me to close my eyes. "Mom," I started, "why do I need to close my eyes when all the presents are wrapped?" A widespread smile spread across her face.

"Well, not *all* of them are wrapped, so sit on the couch and close your eyes and hold out your hands."

I did as I was told and impatiently held out my arms. I heard the rustling of paper and felt a box placed in my lap. The box started to move. I opened my eyes and suppressed a scream. I stared at the box a second or two before someone yelled, "Open the lid." Cautiously I lifted the loose lid to see a tiny brown and white Chihuahua puppy with a red bow around her neck. She was looking straight up at me with her big, brown eyes. I looked down at her and then over to my parents. That's when I got really emotional. As my eyes filled with tears, I giggled as I took her out of the box and held her against my chest. "She's so cute," I gushed. "What a total surprise. I didn't even ask for a dog!"

Mom looked over at me and said, "We know you didn't ask. You can thank your sister, Lauren, for asking."

When I looked at Lauren, her face was filled with content. "They said 'no' several times, but I knew you needed one."

Dad nodded, and reiterated, "Yeah, it was Lauren's persistence that got us thinking seriously about it. I told her 'no' five times, but she insisted you needed a dog."

I ran over to Lauren and lifted her off the ground to give her a big hug. I said, "Thank you so much. You knew—you knew!"

It was no secret to either of my sisters that I was living a recluse life and maybe needed something to take my attention away from whatever was bothering me. This little puppy became my constant companion and the surprises from my sisters didn't stop there.

After we finished opening gifts and eating breakfast, we visited in the living room by the Christmas tree. As I took my gifts to my room to put them away I heard something that made me stop in my tracks. "We're going to the Russells this afternoon to do a small gift exchange," Mom announced.

"We should just hang out here and watch a movie," I begged.

"We can't be rude," Mom replied. "I already told them we were coming. Just come for a little bit, and then you can go when you want. You know Jake is excited to see you."

I sighed and under my breath murmured, "Fine, just for a little bit."

I drove myself to the Russells and showed up later than Mom, Dad, Stephanie, and Lauren. Jake and I spent some good quality time together. We visited in the game room, played pool, and snacked on Christmas cookies. When Jake decided to leave the game room to get more milk, I followed close behind.

When I trailed back into the living room, I could see everyone was accounted for. So I left the group and headed to the kitchen to get another Christmas treat. Mr. Russell followed me. As I darted away from him, he said, "I heard you got a new little friend for Christmas. I knew you were getting her. It was hard for me not to say anything." Mid-chew with a cookie, I kept moving and ignored him.

"Well, we should schedule a time to meet now that you have a phone and can drive. How come you haven't been answering my calls?" Without giving me time to answer, he said, "When we meet I can bring some drinks if you want."

I glanced toward the living room to see if anyone had heard his remarks before I said, "I don't think so."

I quickly returned to the game room where Jake was setting up a video game. Cheerful, he glanced at me and said, "We're all going to see a movie tonight. Do you want to go?"

My Christmas spirit deflated. I wanted to see a movie with Jake and everyone else, but not with Mr. Russell. "Sorry Jake, I made plans with Erica for later." It was a lie. I couldn't be around that certain man anymore.

I went home by myself Christmas evening. I was done with all the shame, secrets, and acting.

I had long forgotten the incident with Stephanie on the stairs during Thanksgiving break, but I was soon to learn that she lived with and analyzed the rage I displayed when I yelled at her. In fact, she said it bothered her so much it was difficult to concentrate while studying for her finals.

The day after Christmas I was up before Stephanie in the morning. When I returned from the bathroom, making myself ready for the day, I walked back into the bedroom to see Stephanie sitting on the bed, stretching her arms and yawning. I smiled, and she yawned again. She turned a sleepy face toward me and said, "Hey, you want to have lunch with me today? We can go wherever you want."

"Yeah, let's do it!" I missed her so much. At that time, my favorite restaurant was the Neiman Marcus Café. It was a place we went for special occasions. I couldn't know that Stephanie had our day together carefully planned.

The spirit of Christmas was still in the air at the restaurant. When we sat down I asked a lot of questions about her plans for the next semester. She talked about classes and adjusting more to living away from home. She seemed distant when talking about school, and it was easy to tell she wasn't much into the conversation. After we ordered our food, she cleared her throat, straightened up in her chair, and assumed a serious, intent look about her face.

"Jenna, I'm going to ask you an important question that's been on my mind for a while. But, before I say anything, I want you to promise to tell me the truth. Can you do that?" I thought, *Why do I need to promise? Did I put her shirt I borrowed back in her closet? Maybe she noticed I wore her new shoes without asking.* After hesitating I said, "Sure, why would I lie to you about anything?" Even before she could ask the question, I felt tense, almost like the room was closing in on me.

She rested her elbows on the table, leaned toward me, looked directly into my eyes, and said, "Jenna, has anyone ever hurt you?" I couldn't help what happened next. Uncontrollable tears filled my eyes. I didn't even have time to hold back the flow. I lost it right then and there. The server avoided refilling our water, and the whole restaurant could hear me.

She seemed calm and let me cry for a few moments. When I realized others noticing my unruly tears, I regained my composure as quickly as I could. It became obvious to me she already knew the answer before I could say anything. I couldn't keep the tremor from my words, "Yes, but I can't tell you who it is. You know this person well, and you wouldn't believe me."

She refused to accept that for an answer. Shaking her head and in a deep tone of voice, she said, "Oh, no, you're *going* to tell me. You're not going to say someone has hurt you and not say who. We aren't leaving here until you tell me." That's when I knew I wasn't getting out of there without explaining the whole story. I stared at her with a long pause, inhaled a deep breath, and slowly exhaled. I knew this was really it. *Maybe this was something bigger than any of us could survive?*

"OK—it's Mr. Russell," I blurted out. "He's been doing things to me." After taking a sip of water from the table I sat back and fearfully waited for her response.

Her jaw dropped and hung in place while she stared straight at me. Then her hands went to her mouth as she continued her stare. Her eyes grew larger and larger, until I thought they would pop right out of her head.

At last, still hiding her face, she whispered, "Oh, my gosh, I'm so sorry."

It took her time to process what I had said. I was equally in disbelief that I finally exposed Mark Russell after years of being afraid to tell. I remained silent, although I was jittery as I waited for her to speak. She kept shaking her head as she looked down at the table. After what seemed like a long time, just staring at each other, she sat up straight, and, with authority in her voice, she said, "OK, well, we're going to get you help. He is never going to hurt you again."

I tried a few feeble words of refusal, knowing all along that her mind was set.

After recalling the threats from Mr. Russell, my thoughts then shifted to the terror of disappointing Mom and Dad. They worked hard all our lives to keep us safe from the very thing I encountered. I wanted to protect them from the inevitable feelings of betrayal—just a little longer. Desperate, I tried again to prolong the heartbreak and agony that was sure to come, explaining, "I don't want to tell Mom and Dad right now. I would rather wait until I'm graduated and out of school."

She wouldn't have any part of my argument.

"No way, I am *not* going to continue to allow this. I'll help you, Jenna. He won't hurt you again. He needs to know that what he's done is wrong. Just think," she continued, "he's living a great life totally at your expense. He thinks he's getting away with it, too. He knows, and he could care less that he's destroying your life, causing pain and suffering to his family and yours. As of now, that's going to stop!"

Before we left the restaurant, Stephanie wanted to be sure I knew that none of this was my fault. "I know the guilt you might have to work through, but you *must* come to realize that none of this was your doing."

What a dose of reality. She is so right. Why didn't I think about it that way? We smiled at each other across the table and pushed our chairs back. Stephanie didn't want to wait another second. I agreed. We left part of our meal on the table and drove straight home. On the drive home I was reminded of my prayer on Christmas Eve. *Was this the miracle I prayed for?*

My family never called an official meeting before. It just wasn't our style. We talked openly about things. Mom and Dad indulged us and optimistically welcomed our assertiveness. As far as they knew, there was no reason to remotely envision that our meeting would unimaginably change our lives forever.

CHAPTER 13

We all gathered in the living room, except for Lauren. Mom situated Lauren in her room on some project and told her to stay there until our discussion was finished. I sat on the couch next to Steph. She sat next to Mom. Dad sat on my other side. My palms were sweaty, and I could feel my heart with every beat. My thoughts swirled in a cloud of disbelief that the moment I had put off and dreaded for what felt like most my life was finally here.

I was terrified—not for myself, but for the pain and hurt that my parents were about to experience. What I was about to say would change so many lives. Dad and Mom might lose their friends, while Stephanie and I might both lose our best friends. Questions ran through my head. *How will they take the news? What happens next?*

Stephanie helped me by opening the meeting. "Jenna has something very important she wants to tell us." Then she looked over at me and held my hands in support. My mouth was dry. I still couldn't find words. Steph nodded her head and encouraged me. "It's OK. They need to know."

Mom and Dad's faces grew troubled, while I struggled to get

out the first word. Finally, in a calm voice Stephanie said, "Someone has been hurting Jenna." They paled and looked as though they had just seen a ghost. I wondered if they could hear my heart beating.

Mom was the first to react, "Who? Jenna, what's going on?"

Now it was my turn to speak because Mom turned red in the face and stood in a fighting stance. That's when I finally found the courage to speak.

"You're not going to believe me, but it's—it's Mr. Russell."

She gasped and spoke, almost under her breath, "No. No. No. No." Dad was stoic at first, and then he broke down into tears. He stood, moved in front of me, and went to his knees. He called my name, "Jenna . . ." Then he looked down at the floor and wept. He could not find the words.

"How many times, Jenna?" Mom struggled with the words.

My heart jumped into my throat. *Oh, God,* I thought. "I, I don't know, Mom. It's been going on for years." My throat got tight, and I could feel my cheeks getting wet.

Mom opened her mouth, as if to speak, but no words came out. Then, coming from deep down, she said, "What? Jenna, this can't be. Why didn't you tell us? You know you can tell us anything."

Without saying another word Dad stood, walked to the closet, put on his coat, and started toward the door. My worst fears were now confirmed. *Dad was going to take matters into his own hands*—one reason, among many that I had feared the worst about exposing Mr. Russell's abuse. Dad was a man of strong, Christian, personal, and civic convictions, and a man to get his point across in as few words as possible.

Standing five feet ten inches, plus, and weighing about 190 pounds, he had the look, demeanor, and personality of a gentle statesman. But, a casual acquaintance wouldn't know Dad's fierce, competitive athleticism, or that he had been a first-string high school football player and attended college on a baseball scholarship. Nor would the casual acquaintance know that he was the kindest, most loving family man most anyone ever met—always helping strangers and others in need. Putting all of this Teddy bear personality aside, little could Mr. Russell know that at this very moment in his life he was in danger of facing an unimaginable force that would be his worst nightmare.

Mom and Stephanie rushed to stop Dad, stepping in front of him before he could open the door. Stephanie said, "No, Dad . . . No! Please! We are going to call the police."

Dad broke in to plead his case. "I'm just going to have some words with him," which we knew was the last thing on his mind.

Stephanie kept pleading for what seemed to me like a long time, saying things, like: "He isn't worth it, Dad. You don't want to go to jail. It's a job for the police."

Finally, Dad cooled down a little and allowed Mom and Stephanie to lead him to the couch. All of this time I'm standing in the middle of the living room, crying aloud, and feeling the tears running down my face.

Sitting on the edge of the couch, Dad's first words were, "Was it here? Was it here that he hurt you?"

"Yes, Dad, right here in this room." I could barely get the words out. My heart was breaking for Dad's grief. Dad buried his face in his hands and cried aloud for the longest time.

Mom wanted facts, but I couldn't give her facts. I was so overwhelmed from their pain and my own poor emotional state that I just couldn't say anymore.

Finally, Dad regained his composure and found his voice. As he fought back his tears, he reassured me, "Jenna, I'm so happy that you told us. I want you to know that we're going to handle this the right way. I want you to see with your eyes what happens to criminals in our society."

Stephanie suggested again that we call the police and make a report. Dad picked up the phone and dialed 911. With a heavy heart he said, "My daughter was assaulted. You need to get out here now before something bad happens."

Mom and Dad both held me tight. They assured me everything was going to be OK. Dad didn't want me to be surprised, so he told me that two police officers were coming to the house to talk to me. Ready or not, I had to give details. This was the moment I had dreaded for so long.

While trying to pull myself together, Stephanie came over and whispered in my ear. "Don't be afraid to tell them everything. They are here to help you, so be as descriptive as you can." She gave me a big, strong hug of reassurance.

I sat on the couch waiting for the police and mentally tried to recall everything that happened over the years. Stephanie grabbed a pen and a piece of paper, suggesting I jot down dates and incidents. Then before I knew it, the doorbell rang.

Two police officers made their way into the house as Dad reiterated why he called them. I was relieved when one of the officers interviewed me in the dining area where my parents couldn't hear. They didn't need to know the horrific details of what happened. I took Stephanie's advice and told them everything regarding Mr. Russell's abuse.

Talking with the police lasted about three hours or longer. After reliving moments in my mind and writing them down, I felt so pent up. When it was all said and done, I thanked the officer who interviewed me. "That's what we're here for," he replied, with compassion in his voice. He told me to call him if I left anything out or remembered something that I didn't mention during the interview.

As we left the dining room and walked into a different living area, the other officer walked toward Dad. He leaned in toward Dad's shoulder and said, "This guy was really sick. He knew what he was doing." Then the other officer gave Mom some pamphlets of victim service information provided by the state. Dad thanked the officers and walked them to the door. This was the first, but not my last, interview with the police.

Slight relief was soon met with disappointment when I found out that I needed to make a separate statement for the assault Mr. Russell committed in his home. Although the Russells lived less than ten minutes away, they were in a different city. This meant I had to give a second report to the officers in that city. In order to file this second report, I had to physically go down to the police station and write out my statement. My parents drove me there the next morning.

I wrote out as much as I could remember, handed it to the officers, and asked if there was anything else I needed to do. One of the officers explained that I needed a Sexual Assault Nurse Examination (SANE) to help with the investigation. They also said investigators would contact me for further questions. Detectives from the two cities would work on the case together. One of the officers said, after the SANE examination, we would just have to wait for the investigation to be completed before anything else could move further.

To my surprise I learned that not all hospitals had SANE examination rooms. The police had specific hospitals where they referred victims for this purpose. Thankfully, my SANE exam was at a hospital close to home. As I was escorted back to a private room, Mom and Dad were shown to a small room where they waited alone. Back in the examination room, a total stranger was about to analyze my private areas.

The examination room seemed to get smaller by the minute as the nurse asked me to change into a hospital gown. When the nurse walked back in, she said something that made me feel a little better. "It's a good thing you told. You're brave to be here." I nodded, took a deep breath, and muttered, "Thank you." Lying on the table staring up at the bare, white ceiling, I tried to relax as much as possible while she proceeded with the exam. "OK, now on to the hard part, just try to relax."

Finally, after what felt like an incredibly long period of time, my examination was over. The nurse walked with me back to the waiting room. Mom immediately placed some reading material on a nearby coffee table and stood to greet me. Dad looked up and then rose to hug me.

It was a small, cozy-feeling room, and empty except for us. I was looking at the door, ready to walk out, when Mom touched my arm and said, "Wait a minute Jenna. I want to show you something." She retrieved her reading material from the table and pointed to a rack of pamphlets on the wall. "You won't believe what I've been reading."

That's when she handed me a small pamphlet, with one single sheet listing the symptoms of child sexual abuse. I was astounded and couldn't take my eyes off that little sheet of paper.

"Jenna," Mom said, holding the pamphlet before my face, "at one time or another the past few years you have shown almost all of these symptoms. I can't believe it. If I only knew the information on this little piece of paper, I could've saved you sooner from all this. I'm so ashamed and embarrassed I didn't know." She started to tear up. "Where have I been? Where has everybody been?" She explained that in her twenty years of teaching she had never seen any literature in schools that helped teachers identify sexual abuse.

Mom retrieved several copies of the pamphlet. She gave me my own copy, which I folded and stuffed into my purse. After all these years, I still have that list of symptoms tucked away in my bound journal. Below is an updated version of warning signs and possible indicators that a child who is a victim of sexual abuse may display:

CHILDHELP SPEAK UP BE SAFE

Physical indicators

- Has difficulty walking or sitting

- Has a sudden weight change

- Has frequent somatic complaints, stomach or headache, sore throat

- Suddenly refuses to change for gym or to participate in physical activities

- Has sudden negative change in appearance

- Has frequent urinary tract or yeast infections not explained by medical condition or treatment

- Becomes pregnant or contracts a venereal disease, particularly if under age fourteen

- Runs away

Behavioral indicators

- Shows sudden changes in behavior or school performance
- Is inappropriately seductive
- Has sophisticated knowledge or interest in sexual activity and behaviors beyond same age peers
- Perpetrates sexual activity with another child, particularly a younger or more vulnerable child
- Is overly protective of siblings
- Avoids a specific person without an obvious reason
- Talks a lot about an adult
- Is threatened by physical contact, closeness
- Is always watchful, as though preparing for something bad to happen
- Comes to school early, stays late, and does not want to go home

Additional indicators for adolescents

- Is self-destructive
- Is considered promiscuous
- Abuses drugs or alcohol
- Self mutilates or attempts suicide
- Develops an eating disorder

DARKNESS TO LIGHT
STEWARDS OF CHILDREN

- Blame themselves for the abuse

- Feel guilty or dirty

- Feel hopeless

- Fear even healthy affection

- Feel angry and disconnected from others

- Feel that others don't really know them

- Feel like they will never be OK

- Doubt that they can take care of themselves

- Have illnesses and body sensations that are traumatizing

- Feel powerless

- Live in secrecy

- Feel trapped

- Forget things that have happened

- Feel tremendous shame

- Hate themselves

- Put themselves in dangerous situations

- Get in trouble to show how "bad" they are or to call attention to their trauma

- Fear being close to others, even in friendships

- Be afraid of being "found out"

- Experience memories, pictures, smells, and sounds that are re-traumatizing

- Feel fearful even during times that are "safe"

- Startle easily

- Have nightmares or fear going to sleep

- Feel abandoned by parents and family

- Lost hope and trust in other people

- Feel unloved by God

- Feel they aren't worthy of being loved

The day after Christmas and the weeks that followed were emotionally draining for us. No one slept well. Talking about the abuse and then having to write about it in statements was like living it all over again. It was supposed to make me feel better. It didn't. It was like going through everything all over again in real time. Except this time it wasn't just me being victimized. My whole family was on fire, all of us living the hell I had experienced.

CHAPTER 14

Every Christmas break my school participated in an annual basketball tournament with other Christian schools. Our first game was against Oak Ridge Academy in Arlington, Texas, about twenty miles from our school. This was the biggest tournament of the year. My family and the Russells all attended. I played for the girls' high school varsity, and Jake played for the boys' high school varsity. The tournament was touted as a good prediction for how we would perform in the district playoffs. Mr. and Mrs. Russell and Jackie would be at the tournament to watch us compete.

This would be the first time my family had seen the Russells since Mr. Russell was exposed at our family meeting. Mr. Russell had not been informed that he was a suspect, and the police investigators told us *not to say anything* to the Russells during the initial investigation. They emphasized that we should stay completely away from any contact with them, if at all possible. On a chance meeting, my parents were to go on as if everything was normal.

Before we started for the game we had a brief family meeting in our living room. We joined hands and asked God's help to see us through what we hoped would be our last close-up encounter with this family before a decision was made by the police. But, even with all of our mental preparation, I wondered how Dad could possibly handle such a situation. Also, my biggest concern was how Mom would keep herself together.

While warming up for the game on the basketball court I spotted Mr. Russell with his wide, friendly smile walking toward me from the other side of the gym. Wanting to disappear right then and there, I prayed to God under my breath he wouldn't give me his customary hug or "pep talk" before the game. He didn't hug me, but he put his arm around my shoulder and asked, "Are you ready to play?" I ignored him. Despite my show of indifference, he kept his arm around my shoulder and continued his monologue, none of which remained with me.

I shrugged him off and made a dash toward the locker room. Then I felt a familiar nausea pain in the pit of my stomach.

Mom and Dad arrived to our first game of the tournament to learn the Russells were already there. Grace was seated in the bleachers, but Mark Russell was still on the floor with the players, who were warming up. Mr. Russell wasn't our coach and didn't belong on the gym floor. Disgustingly, he always made a big showing before all our high school games, like he was an important part of the team when he was no more involved than any other parent. Mom and Dad spotted Grace right away and found a place to sit, several seats away.

While running my team warm-up drills, I kept a sharp eye on what was happening in the bleachers. It wasn't long before Grace got up from her seat and moved to sit next to Mom. Then Dad rose from his seat for an apparent phone call and moved toward the restroom.

It wasn't long then before my eyes caught Mr. Russell walking off the gym floor toward the spectator section where he belonged. He seated himself next to Dad who had returned to his seat. Immediately Dad put the phone to his ear and made another restroom visit.

Our team was scheduled to play two games, win or lose. In my state of mind, I didn't care who won or lost either game. My sights were on Dad, fearing he would lose control and we would be bailing him out of jail before the first game even started.

From the start of the game I didn't play well, which didn't set me in good standing with the spectator coach, Mr. Russell, who came over to where I was sitting on the bench during half time. As I took a drink of Gatorade, he crouched down in front of me, in a very coach-like stance. I turned partway around and saw Dad leaning forward, with his elbows on his knees, looking straight at us. There was no question in my mind that he was just waiting for one inappropriate touch by Mr. Russell and he would be on the gym floor in less than a minute, committing the unthinkable. I couldn't let that happen. I smiled and waved at him.

Mr. Russell glanced back to see where I was looking. Then he turned his attention back to me and said, "What's wrong with you? I haven't seen you play this bad, ever!" He asked if there was anything he could do to help.

I shouted back, "I don't need your advice! Just let me play."

He shook his head in disgust and walked away. *Seriously?! If he only knew why my head was not in the game, and if he only knew I had just saved an old man from total physical destruction.*

During that game, I scored less than ten points, which was a poor showing for a forward. Our whole team played poorly, and we finished the tournament somewhere close to last place.

A week went by, then two weeks, with no news about how the investigation was progressing. Since the investigation was taking place between Christmas and New Year, we assumed that part of the staff was on vacation.

Passage of time wore heavily on Mom and Dad. I had never seen them so down. The whole atmosphere reminded me of a showing at a mortuary. They ate very little and slept hardly at all. I guess the symptoms of depression would describe all of our immediate family. Mom seemed to be the most affected, often crying or wiping tears. Even with her own oppression and sadness, Mom, through mostly prayer and meditation, was the one that kept calm and stayed the most positive in our family.

The week school started back after Christmas break I stayed home from school, sick. Mom also took the week off from teaching to stay home with me. Toward the end of the week that Mom and I were away from school, Dad received the long awaited call. I saw his countenance change to a glimmer of hope on his face, the first sign of hope in a very long time. He looked at me with the phone to his ear and gave me the thumbs up. Mike King, one of the police investigators, was on the line.

Mom and I were just starting a conversation when Dad returned to the kitchen. "Mike King is on hold," he said. "He needs to ask you a couple of questions about the case they're building." He handed me the phone, and I walked to Lauren's room to speak privately.

It was a short interview, with only two questions. After thanking me for taking the call, King asked, "Is there anything else that you want to tell us that you didn't get a chance to tell the police in the other interviews?"

"Well, I may not have told you that he called me several times on my cell phone, asking if I would meet him in secret someplace and described sexual things he wanted to do to me."

"OK," he said. "Now you mentioned in a prior conversation with us that you received a certain gift from Mark Russell for your birthday. Do you still have that item?"

"Absolutely not. The 'gift' you referred to was something he slipped into my gym bag without my knowledge. I wrapped the filthy thing in a plastic bag and threw it into the trash the minute I discovered it."

"That's all the questions I have for you at this time," he said. "Do you have any questions before I let you go?"

"Just one," I said. "Do you have enough information to charge him?"

"We think we have enough. Thanks for your cooperation," he said, with what I thought was strong conviction in his voice.

At first I was reluctant and embarrassed to reveal the ugly details of Mr. Russell's attacks to a near stranger on the phone. I had to keep reminding myself that Stephanie had cautioned me not to hold back when questioned. Her small piece of advice helped because it allowed me to feel more secure and confident that I was doing the right thing. The "right thing"—I had to keep reminding myself, just to keep an ounce of sanity.

Dad reminded me that two police departments were working together to build the case. "They are going to charge him soon. It won't be long," he said. I wanted to believe him, but I also didn't want to be disappointed. Mr. Russell fooled so many people. *How successful will he be in getting himself out of this?*

Almost two weeks had passed since we called 911. During that period of time we anxiously waited and prayed for a time of resolution.

At first Mom assured me, "No one outside of our house is going to find out what happened to you, no one." We have a large and close extended family scattered from the southern borders of Texas to the northern borders of Colorado. Keeping our secret confined to our immediate locality suited me just fine, but I almost smiled at the impossibility of that idea. It wasn't long before my skepticism proved to be an accurate reaction. My parents were suffering and needed family support. I wasn't told who received the first call, but before many days had passed the phone never quit ringing as family checked in to offer encouragement.

Mom had not yet returned to the classroom but continued to take personal days. I went back to school so I didn't fall too behind in my studies and hoped that no one would find out.

During the second week in January, Mike King called to tell Dad that he had called Mr. Russell and asked him to come in for questioning. Dad said King didn't tell Mr. Russell why it was important for him to come in, and he didn't recall if Mr. Russell had asked him.

Late in the afternoon, the next day, Mike King called Dad again to tell him that Mr. Russell was a "No show" at the police station. He said when they called him a second time Mr. Russell was told he was under arrest for his no show performance, and they strongly advised him to show up at the station as soon as possible, or they would send patrols to look for him.

On Friday, January 9, 2004, Mr. Russell walked into the police station, accompanied by his attorney. Finally, right there at the station Mark Russell was charged with five counts of indecency with a child and two counts of sexual assault. His attorney tried but couldn't stop the arrest because an arrest warrant had already been issued. We were told he was arrested the minute he walked into the building and identified himself.

When Dad relayed the news to me, he was wiping tears from his cheeks.

Since the beginning of the police involvement in my case, even though her husband had caused indescribable pain and heartache to our household, it was important to my parents that Grace realized we still cared and supported her and her children.

The day that Mike King called to tell Dad an arrest warrant had been issued for Mark Russell, I was at school and then at basketball practice. When I arrived home after basketball practice, I found Mom and Dad sitting at the kitchen table, in what appeared to be a serious discussion, but I didn't want to let on that I noticed. Casually, I said, "Hi, Dad, Mom. What's happening?"

Mom came to her feet as I tossed my backpack onto the couch. "Hi, Honey," she said. "Sit down with us, and we'll tell you all about our less than pleasant day."

Dad was sitting at his usual place at the end of the table, staring at an empty coffee cup, elbows on the table, hands under his chin. Mom started off, "I called Grace today and asked her to stop over on her way home from work. We assumed that she knew all about Mark's arrest and booking, and we felt a real need to tell her our side of the story."

With tears starting to come now, Mom was barely able to continue. "I wish I could relate all the emotions, and our word-for-word conversation. Mark had not told Grace anything. She was so appalled, I thought she was going to pass out, and your dad and I weren't in much better shape. Grace was in such indescribable shock, she couldn't say a word. She buried her face in her hands and kept repeating, 'NO, NO, NO, NO.' When she was able to collect herself, she pushed herself out of the chair and said, 'I gotta go.' Grace was pushing numbers on her phone before she even opened the door to go outside. It was a short moment before we heard her screaming, at what we guessed, was someone she had called."

CHAPTER 15

Learning that Mr. Russell made bail caused his arrest to feel like a short-term victory. Considering his past actions that stemmed from a lack of good judgment, arrogance, and a self-serving nature, we didn't know what harm he might try to inflict upon any one of our family members. The fact that he lived around the corner from us didn't help our feelings of uncertainty. He had declared his innocence and was determined to fight.

The day after Mr. Russell's arrest, the school atmosphere changed significantly. Overnight my peers distinguished me as a deviant, someone who had willingly, or otherwise, had a long-time secret sexual relationship with a man old enough to be my granddad. Even my friends and classmates acknowledged me with lowered heads and whispered greetings when we passed in the hallway, labeling me as someone to be avoided. I was an outcast of the worst kind, feeling like they could all see right through me, and didn't like what they saw.

Attending school each day began to feel like a life sentence in prison. I conjured up my own monologues about what they were saying: "Poor Mr. Russell. He's such a nice guy to go to jail, and all because of Jenna. Who would have thought she was that kind of a person, anyway?"

Socially, I was living in a vacuum. No one wanted to get too close to me for fear of getting sucked into my world. Teachers didn't know *how* to be encouraging or supportive about my experience with sexual abuse. I felt a lack of concern or encouragement everywhere. It was as if some of my worst fears came true and my life was devastatingly worse since I told.

Most days, I stayed in bed and told my parents I was too sick to go to school. At first they let me stay home a few times because they knew how I was treated. When they finally made me go to school, I often saw the school nurse. She allowed me to sleep on a cot for a couple of hours since I mentioned I didn't sleep well most nights and developed severe headaches during the day.

More times than I can count, I suffered from night terrors that came upon me with no notice. Suddenly, I would wake up in a cold sweat, out of breath, and somehow jump out of my bed and make it halfway down the stairs to the landing. When I fully reached consciousness I noticed my hand on the stair railing and felt my heart beating out of my chest. It took me hours to get my heart rate down after experiencing a night terror. To help with the fear, I slept with my closet light on every night—something I wasn't proud of at age sixteen. By the time the sun came up in the morning, I was sick to my stomach. Lack of sleep, coupled with severe anxiety, made me nauseous throughout the day.

Truancy, which led to lower grades, lack of motivation, low self-esteem, and no will to survive put me in a freefall. I had a couple of concerned teachers who contacted Mom about my rapidly falling grades. However, Mom was also in survival mode at the school as a staff member. She was struggling to fight her own battles at school and found it difficult to fight on two fronts.

My algebra teacher showed the most care. Mr. Kinney was an ex-marine, with a reputation for being the toughest teacher on campus. He was a huge, hulking, intimidating, seemingly unapproachable man. He looked to be in his mid-forties, with a bushy head of dark brown hair that he struggled to keep in place. He rarely smiled, and his teaching methods reflected his personality—dry. He insisted on total concentration during class, and he refused to accept excuses for late homework.

When my grades started dropping he asked me to come in for tutoring during lunch hour or after school. He assured me that I would get better grades if I would accept his help. As fractured as my spirits and energy were, I was thankful to be offered help with math. I knew very well if I didn't pass algebra I would be forced to retake the course during summer school. At the time I had no idea how many hours I would spend with Mr. Kinney in intense tutoring or how it would help me.

Attending Bible classes and memorizing verses on a daily basis were momentary releases from stress, but it all seemed to be a contradiction between what I believed to be true about God and what was happening in my life. I felt totally unworthy of love, and nothing I was being told or read seemed to apply to me.

Mom and Dad seemed to be at the breaking point when they finally reached out to a psychiatric clinic for help, maybe hoping for a miracle that their constant prayers hadn't yet delivered. None of my family had ever visited with a psychiatrist. Prayer was their answer to just about everything. Even though I understood that Mom and Dad were praying for me practically nonstop, they weren't seeing immediate results, and I had to assume they felt God could use a doctor's skill.

On an overcast February morning my parents and I arrived at the psychiatric clinic a half-hour early, as instructed. The building looked like a small hospital, and I remarked as much to my parents. Mom reached over and took my sweaty hand in hers, and told me not to worry. "There will be no needles or embarrassing physical exams." But, there *were* pages and pages of forms to fill out. Mom and I both worked on the questions, finishing long after I gave up and hoped to just leave and go home.

Finished with the written part, I was shown to a single room to wait alone where I walked around reading awards and degrees hanging in large frames covering most of four walls. The degrees, I supposed, were to give authenticity to the man appointed to save me from my wreckage. At the time, I was holding out less hope from this stranger than I had received from my fervent prayers. *After all,* I reasoned, *if God can't save me, and I can't save myself, what chance does a stranger with a dozen degrees and awards (all from colleges I'd never heard of) have of saving me?*

I was still trying to pronounce names of strange sounding medical colleges when I heard a slight knock. The door opened and a man wearing a white coat moved toward me. The man who offered me a handshake was rather small-statured, clean shaven and unsmiling. His complexion and facial features reminded me of other doctors I had visited in the Dallas Metro area. We exchanged names, but I forgot his name as quickly as he said it, and I still can't remember it. He remained unsmiling, not at all friendly, and I got the impression he was going to spend the rest of our time together deciding if he liked me.

He asked me to relax in one of the soft leather chairs, while he pulled up a hardback chair with wheels to face me. With not many words wasted on how the interview would be conducted, he started right in with the purpose of this visit.

"Have you ever tried to hurt yourself?" he asked, while looking down at his notepad.

"Sometimes I cut myself."

"Why would you cut yourself?" he asked.

"It makes me feel better."

"OK," he said.

Then came the biggie: "Have you ever thought about taking your own life?"

I sat back in my chair and looked at the floor, trying to convince myself to be honest with this stranger, and wondering at the same time how the truth would set with my parents. I kept my eyes on the floor, but I could feel his eyes boring right through me. Finally, I said, "Yes, I have thought about it."

"How?" he asked.

"Well, Dad keeps a gun in his drawer near the bed for self-defense. If I shot myself in the head it would be quick." I was stuttering.

His last question was, "Can you be absolutely honest with me and tell me all of your symptoms, I mean, why you are here today?"

"Yes, I can be honest." I spent the rest of the interview pouring out all of my anxieties—how telling seemed to make my everyday life worse. And answered more questions.

After my one-on-one with the psychiatrist, we switched and my parents talked to him as I waited outside his office. On the way home, my parents told me the psychiatrist said I had symptoms of post-traumatic stress disorder, severe depression, anxiety, insomnia, and suicidal ideation. I didn't know what "ideation" meant, but the other words on the list didn't come as a surprise.

He prescribed me three types of medication. The first was an antidepressant. I was to gradually take more milligrams over time to get the highest dosage available. Next, he prescribed medication for insomnia to be taken every night before bed. Last was antianxiety medication because I was suffering from flashbacks.

The psychiatrist also told my parents to remove the handgun from the house. Mom and Dad's response was typical: "I can't believe my ears." They kept the weapon hidden and thought I didn't know where it was. They were also shocked to learn that I had considered taking my own life. They vowed to do everything in their power to help me.

Mom and Dad took turns carefully monitoring my prescriptions and kept them in their possession at all times. They also removed Dad's gun. That afternoon, Dad saw a note on the prescription labels indicating they shouldn't be taken on an empty stomach. He knew I hadn't eaten. So, he cooked my favorite homemade biscuits to allow me to follow the prescription directions.

Early that evening, I ate half a biscuit, swallowed a half-pill, and then walked upstairs and rolled into my bed to monitor the effects of the pills. It didn't seem long before I developed an appetite. After wandering downstairs, Mom and Dad were eager to know how I felt. I finished eating my biscuits and returned to bed.

Other than the increase in appetite, my symptoms didn't get any better, despite maintaining a regular pill dosing routine. Every area of my life reflected and reminded me of the past. At times I thought I was going crazy, or maybe I was already crazy, just waiting for a trip to the nuthouse (that's what I called it). In the beginning I had no idea things would get so complicated. In my own mind everything seemed so methodical and simple: The man was guilty. He had been arrested and would be dealt with. He would no longer be a part of anything associated with my life.

Wrong, again. This whole thing felt like it had turned into a fiasco; a nightmare for me and what seemed like at least a hundred other people. At times I wished I could just go back to being a victim and then my family would still be happy and blissfully unaware as Mr. Nice Guy blessed the food before we ate. Before telling, my peers didn't treat me different, I didn't have to go to multiple counseling sessions, and my grades weren't as poor from missed days of school. At other times I thought: *If only I could just disappear and not have to think of it anymore....*

Mark Russell made bail in about the time it would take to order and drink a Starbucks latte. It seemed he was living a free and easy life. Since his arrest I had plenty of time to think about the torture he put me through. Even with all the hassle and sleepless nights, my mind was finally made up. I was going to see the court process through, even if I went crazy in the process. I never told anyone about my resolve.

My parents soon realized I was not healing even with the prescriptions and counseling sessions. In fact, I was regressing. They tried every option they knew available. I was getting regular care from a highly rated psychologist and psychiatrist in the Dallas Metro. Despite my efforts and the efforts of others around me, something was missing. I felt empty and alone, and continued to self-soothe by cutting. My parents couldn't bear to watch me self-mutilate. Each time they begged me to stop, I replied, "It's not that easy to stop." Cutting was the only thing that helped me manage my pain. "I'm not hurting anyone, just myself," I told them.

When they could stand it no longer, Mom and Dad followed me to my room at bedtime one evening and gave me their decision. "Jenna," Mom said, "we're out of options. Tomorrow I'll call your psychiatrist and ask to have you admitted to Green Oaks Mental Hospital. We'll no longer stay still and watch you slowly destroy yourself."

While I agreed to voluntarily stay in psychiatric care, my biggest concern was that, once they checked me in, I was not allowed to voluntarily leave. The facility and the professionals in it had exclusive rights as to when I could be released from their care. Despite these concerns, we all agreed that this was the best option for me because I could not control my self-harm. Once we made that agreement, I started packing.

After only a few minutes of packing, Lauren stepped into my room. She stood at the foot of my bed for several minutes, watching me fold clothes and place them into a suitcase. "You're leaving?" she asked, with a quiet voice. "You're leaving?" she repeated. In the middle of folding one of my shirts, I stopped what I was doing and whispered, "Yes, I'm going somewhere for a little while, but then I'm coming back." She nodded with what seemed to be a worried look and then asked, "Are you going to be here to make cupcakes for my birthday? Every year we make them to share with my class remember?" Her thirteenth birthday was only a couple of days away, on February 26.

She touched a place in my heart I forgot existed. I had been so self-serving lately. It was *her* birthday, and *she needed me to be her sister.* I cracked a smile, and for a moment my world seemed orderly again. I hesitated to answer. She looked up at me with a stare, waiting for my reply. My little sister adored me, and I wasn't about to let her down if I could help it. So, I tried to give her some hope and responded, "I think I might stay. Let me see what I can do."

As I walked downstairs to talk with Mom, I noticed Lauren followed close behind me. "Mom, Lauren needs me. I should stay for our cupcake baking." Mom was not easily convinced.

"You just told me that you couldn't stop hurting yourself. I can't let you do that," she replied. Then I promised her that I wouldn't harm myself for Lauren's birthday. I pleaded. She agreed that one more day was OK.

The next day, Lauren and I enjoyed baking together. We listened to music, danced with our aprons on, and made a mess in the kitchen mixing the cupcake batter together. She didn't see me differently or treat me differently. Her company was easy, and our conversations were simple. Just as Stephanie was there for me when I needed her, helping Lauren was a responsibility that gave me purpose. I wasn't alone. I had my sisters.

Baking cupcakes with Lauren allowed me to get through more than just one extra day outside Green Oaks; it was the beginning of a temporary, renewed sense of resolve. After a long private conversation with Mom that same evening, it was settled. Early the next morning, Mom called and canceled my appointment with Green Oaks.

Mom was convinced that I could do this. And I was just as convinced and determined. *I was not going to let her down.* I had to fight harder to heal, not only for myself, but for those who loved me as well. I had to hold on to that moment.

CHAPTER 16

If the district attorney accepted my case, I would face Mr. Russell in the courtroom. I would have to take the stand, look him straight in the face, and identify him as the man who assaulted me. It was explained to me that I would have to tell everything, and I mean . . . *everything. How could I possibly do this in front of the jury, the judge, my grandpa, aunts, uncles, and all my supporters and friends?*

Over and over I was told how important my testimony was to the case. My worst fear, aside from the case being dismissed, was my own mental state. *Was I brave enough to take the stand and tell the truth about all the horrible things he put me through?* All of these threats to my emotional capacity came to a head on the last day of February 2004 when a letter arrived from the district attorney. The letter read: "In the above case, the Grand Jury voted to True Bill criminal charges against the accused. This means our office will prosecute the case."

The day after the police report was initially filed, a woman from the police department called to tell my parents about the

Children's Advocacy Center in Denton County (CACDC). Mom and Dad eventually decided to look into their services. I wasn't happy about having to go to a new therapeutic facility. I was already going to two different facilities; one for the psychiatric visits and one for the psychologist visit, not to mention all the support and well-intended advice I gathered from loved ones and others.

Telling my story over and over to well-meaning professionals, who were total strangers in the beginning, was mentally and physically exhausting. It was getting to a point where I could barely concentrate on my own responses and their knowledgeable advice. I was convinced that all the people in these clinics were right in their assessment and advice, but not much of it was sticking. I was still a nervous wreck and scared half to death. It was easy to see that my parents were excited about me visiting the CACDC and I guessed they were expecting the same response from me, which wasn't the case at all. But when the votes were counted, it was like two wolves and a lamb voting on what's for dinner. I was going.

Dad and Mom drove me to the CACDC for a consultation visit. Not long after we arrived, a therapist came through the door on the other side of the waiting room and greeted us. "I'm Rose," she said in her raspy smoker's voice as she smiled from ear to ear. Rose was an older woman of average height and weight. Her blonde hair was short and she didn't wear a stitch of makeup. After we were introduced and given a short explanation as to our visit, she asked us to follow her for a tour of the facility.

One of the first things I noticed was a wall stacked with shelves filled with teddy bears of different sizes and colors. Rose noticed my special interest in the teddy bears and stopped to explain: "Every child," she said, "who attends the clinic for counseling is allowed to pick out a teddy bear to take home and keep as their own. When they feel unloved or unwanted, they are encouraged to remember the teddy bear and what it represents—a physical reminder of the support offered by the Children's Advocacy Center."

She then pointed to a wall next to the teddy bears where I saw an unfurled roll of white paper with colorful handprints stamped all over. Most of the handprints were much smaller than mine.

She explained that children who had received counseling there made the handprints. When they arrived, they dipped their hand in the paint and then pressed their hand on the white paper next to all the other handprints. Together the many handprints represented a sense of community and belonging. The children could look at all the other handprints and know they were going to be a part of a community of survivors. They were not alone.

She turned to me and said, "Would you like to pick a bear from the wall?" There were so many teddy bears to choose from; I hesitated. I couldn't remember the last time I had a new stuffed teddy bear. Scanning the shelves, I looked for the perfect bear. "This is the one!" I said as I grabbed a soft, medium-sized white bear. "Angel is her name." Rose chuckled. Pleased with my willingness to participate, she then asked if I wanted to put my handprint on the wall. Nodding my head to agree, I handed the bear over to Mom. After Rose dipped my hand in green paint, I slowly pressed my right hand on the white paper near all the other handprints.

We continued the tour and walked into each room that was not being used. There was a conference room, play therapy room, forensic interview room, counseling rooms, and offices for staff.

After the tour, we moved into one of the private rooms with Rose. She talked with my parents, and they discussed the details of my case. Then she asked me which kind of counseling I preferred: one-on-one counseling, group counseling, or both. Not at all feeling ready to talk in a group, I chose one-on-one counseling. Rose recommended I attend counseling twice a week after school.

Going for counseling at the CACDC twice a week was emotionally demanding. Knowing that Mr. Russell was the reason I needed counseling made me angry—not just angry, but an intense, burning resentment that my life was still controlled by a mastermind pervert. These feelings of anger and resentment consumed my whole train of thought until finally, I revolted. Mom was walking with me to my car for moral support as she usually did before I drove to counseling. Except this time, I suddenly stopped and turned to face her. With as much determination as I could muster, I shouted, "I am not going."

Mom's immediate response was a blank stare. I had no way of knowing if she was preparing for an all-out confrontation or some kindly persuasion. Lucky for me, Mom used her customary persuasion tactic. "Honey, you *have* to go. We may be going to court sooner than you think."

Again, I pleaded, "No, I'm *really* not going."

"Get in the car—*right now,*" she said, with more authority than I had ever heard from Mom in my short life.

I started to cry. I didn't exactly know why, but the tears didn't seem to need a reason. Mom let me cry, for what seemed like a long time. Finally, she offered me a cloth to wipe my face, before saying, "Honey, I know this is hard, but it's the best thing for you. You'll see, this will all be behind you soon." I heard her, but I was not listening. Mom approached me, putting her arm around my shoulder. "Let's go Honey. I'll drive you, and you can tell me what's wrong on the way to your session, if you want to. And please talk to the counselor about your feelings."

My counselor looked at me as if she could see I was anxious when I arrived at the CACDC. When she greeted me with that warm smile, I lost it. She remained calm and put her hand on my shoulder saying, "It's OK to cry, let's sit down and talk." When we both sat down in the counseling room, I spoke first: "Sorry, I know this is a great place, but I just don't want to be here." She waited for me to gain my composure before she spoke.

She looked at me and said, "We don't have to talk about anything you don't want to talk about today. If you want to talk about shoes, we can talk about shoes." I wiped my tears and then giggled at her comment. "Well, I like shoes. I just don't get to wear the fun ones thanks to the uniform policy at my school." After we talked for a few more minutes, I opened up to her with why I was so troubled: "I just feel like I shouldn't have to be here in the first place. That dirtbag old man is controlling how I spend my time now that I have to come here."

She listened as she nodded her head in agreement. "No child should ever have to be here. But because they went through something traumatic, they can come here to start healing." She didn't just leave it at that, though. As she talked on, she explained that I was just one of hundreds of children who came to the CACDC for help. "We do our best to let them know that none of the pain and suffering they are experiencing is any of their own fault," she said. Gradually, I started to listen more closely and feel more comfortable in her presence, even to the point of thinking it was a good idea that I went that day.

When I stepped out of the counseling session, I felt a new sense of self-empowerment. The counselor stressed, in so many ways, that I had to see myself as worthy of healing. It took a lot for me to believe I deserved to be whole again. I wanted to be fixed instantly, but it didn't work that way. I was beginning to understand that I had to have the courage to face the challenge with whatever time and effort it took to win the battle. In time, I came to believe the CACDC was a place I could restore my confidence in myself through the healing process they provided. The CACDC offered me the courage to hope for healing and to believe I deserved happiness again. That was my new goal. I dared myself to be happy again.

Feeling self-assured, while we were having our evening meal at home, I openly asked my parents a question: "Why don't you guys go to counseling?"

"Why do we need counseling?" Mom asked.

Looking across the table at Dad, I stopped eating for a time and placed my fork on my plate, "Well, counseling is actually really great. If it's helping me, it should help you."

They stopped what they were doing and looked at each other across the table. Before they could say anything, I reminded them that the CACDC offered free counseling services to non-offending family members, too. "Please just give it a try." My parents needed *something* because they had changed, too, and not for the better. They were both fighting depression. I had several places to go for help, and it seemed they had no place to go. Dad finally broke the silence, "If you want us to go, we'll go."

From that time on, Mom and Dad were regulars during the evening CACDC sessions, and I attended my regular meetings after school. It got to be a regular thing, discussing our counseling sessions until late after each meeting, similar to kindergarten chatter between brothers and sisters after school. They said they enjoyed talking to the other parents and relating to their stories. During the group counseling, they vented and shared their frustrations. In the sessions, they could share what they didn't feel comfortable discussing anywhere else. They said it felt like a big family discussion.

As I continued counseling, the CACDC directed me toward a unique biker group. The name of the group was called B.A.C.A. It stood for Bikers Against Child Abuse. I loved the sound of their name and what they stood for the minute I heard of them. My parents also heard about B.A.C.A. from the parent group. They related that B.A.C.A. members were well known to be there for the abused child whenever they were needed.

From other families at the CACDC meetings, my parents learned that the burly bikers sat with children at the lunch table in school to keep them feeling safe and secure. They also stood near the abused kids' homes at night if a child felt fearful of a perpetrator. They took children to parks and gave them rides on their motorcycles, escorted parents and children to court dates, and stayed in court to support the child during trials. In general, they used their "biker image" to help children who suffered from abuse feel safe and supported.

When I was younger, Dad owned a motorcycle. He didn't keep it very long, though. He got rid of it because he said Mom was starting to get gray hair from so much worry. Also, Dad was giving us girls fun rides, which added more gray hairs to poor old Mom. Now that we were older she backed off her fears a little and allowed an initiation bike ride with the B.A.C.A. group. I guessed she figured she had all the gray hairs allotted to her by then.

We scheduled a meeting on a Saturday morning to visit with members of our nearby B.A.C.A. chapter. I could hear the loud rumblings of their engines when they arrived at our home. When I answered the door, my eyes focused on a woman and a man, both dressed in jeans and black biker vests. Their biker vests had a name across the back. A big red patch read, "B.A.C.A." Inside the B.A.C.A. lettering was a hand in the shape of a fist punch. On the vest were other patches and memorabilia too. We invited them into the house and greeted them with cookies. I couldn't wait to make friends with real bikers.

They both looked intimidating with their well-worn and broken-in vests, patches, jeans, and boots. While munching on cookies, the biker woman approached me, introducing herself with her biker "handle," Armlock. "That's my road name," she said. She turned her back to me so I could read the patches on her vest. The male biker joined in conversation, displaying his road name, "Danno." Staring at his vest, I asked him if that was his real name. He grinned and said, "No, every B.A.C.A. member has a road name that they are known by. We use our road names to protect ourselves and the kids in the group. If you want to become a member of the group, you can choose your own name."

I want my name to be something fearsome. "I like snakes! How about 'Venom' for my road name? That sounds like a cool name."

Startled, Mom turned to me and asked, "What? Since when do you like snakes?!"

"People are afraid of snakes," I responded. I wanted to be feared for a change.

Armlock looked at me and agreed, "Venom. We don't have that name yet. Is that the name you want for sure?"

Yes, I was sure that "Venom" was my biker name. Mom didn't approve, initially, but she saw how excited I was and let it go.

Once I gave them my vest size and road name, we decided to do the adoption on Saturday a few weekends later. They explained that all or most of the B.A.C.A. members in the area attended the adoption. The B.A.C.A. members ride to your house on their motorcycles and present you with your new member vest. This is intended to be a strong public statement. I felt stronger already from my new biker name: "Venom," but, I had no idea what I was in for at the adoption ceremony.

On the Saturday of my adoption I dressed in a black shirt and jeans for the occasion. I could hear them as they approached the house. It sounded like roaring thunder. Dad, Mom, Lauren, and I all ran outside to greet them. As I stood on the steps in front of the house, my heart leaped in excitement. The sound of the engines rumbling was riveting. It sounded as though there were hundreds of B.A.C.A. members. One after the other they rode in.

They didn't have enough room to park all their bikes in our cul-de-sac. So when they parked their bikes at the house, they lined up parallel to each other. Then, I saw Armlock. She had her sunglasses on and smiled at me once she parked her bike. She directed the others to get off their bikes and walk toward me. There must have been at least forty B.A.C.A. members. Once they parked and got off their bikes, they formed a half-circle around the front of our house.

Armlock led the ceremony. One at a time, they said their road names and a little about their backgrounds. They included where they were from and how many years they were part of B.A.C.A. They looked intimidating, but I grew more comfortable around them as they talked about themselves. They gathered in a tighter circle around me as they talked.

After the introductions, Armlock brought out my vest and presented it to me. The vest was black leather and on the upper back was stitched, "Venom" in white letters. She placed the vest over me and spoke about what it meant to be a part of B.A.C.A.

She said B.A.C.A. was available for me if I ever felt threatened by Mr. Russell. She also mentioned that they could accompany me to court. She even offered to come to my school, take me to the park, or give me a motorcycle ride whenever I felt like it.

B.A.C.A. members offered accessories to go along with my vest. One man gave me a du-rag to wear under my helmet when I rode. Another woman gave me her white sport sunglasses to wear on the bike rides. The members took specific pins off their vests and gave them to me, explaining the meaning behind the pin as a gift.

To add to the support, they presented me with a teddy bear. Each member in the circle hugged this "biker" bear and then passed it to the next member to hug. They advised me to hug the bear and remember the adoption when I felt scared or alone. While their support was tangible, I also received a sense of empowerment from the B.A.C.A. members that day. And I really didn't expect such kindness from the rough-looking crowd.

Before the ceremony was over, it was time to take a motorcycle ride. I was told to pick out my favorite bike. As I fought back overwhelming tears of joy, I walked by the row of bikes and picked the one I thought was the loudest—Armlock's bike. Once everyone was back on his or her bike, Armlock gave the signal to go. We were at the front of the line and took off first. One by one, each biker sped out after the other in a synchronized way. I laughed and squealed as we turned corners and traveled down steep hills. It was an incredible feeling to have so many people around that were all there for *me*.

After the ceremony, I wore my vest for the remainder of the day and placed my new biker bear where I could easily see him in my bedroom. I didn't want to forget that day or lose the feeling of encouragement.

As the days wound down toward the trial, I attended extra counseling sessions at the CACDC, preparing for accusations from Mr. Russell's attorney against my character and against my description of the events. As terrified as I was, I felt ready and willing to face a jury, and even Mr. Russell, to tell my story. But that wasn't meant to be—not in the foreseeable future, anyway. Mr. Russell requested and received a continuance of the court date.

A strong feeling of helplessness mixed with frustration engulfed me. No one had explained the possibility of a continuance to me. I had worked so hard to prepare and could feel the pressure building in the coming days to just get it over.

CHAPTER 17

Granting Mark Russell a trial date continuance upset me more than I realized. My progress was discouraging despite rarely missed counseling sessions with my psychologist and regular attendance at the CACDC. It was one step forward and seven steps backward. No matter how hard I tried, my head was never straight enough to put together one action to make life any better. I couldn't concentrate on any one subject for more than a few seconds before going on to another thought.

In the meantime, Mom performed regular checks of my ankles. I tried to disguise my cuts with creams and powders but it didn't work. After her second observation, she stood up, showing a sad face, and said, "Honey, I think it's time we seriously consider admitting you to Green Oaks Mental Hospital."

Standing perfectly still, I took shallow breaths, trying to relax. Knowing that Green Oaks was not a facility for me, I had to think of something to appease Mom for the time being. She continued to look at me with a blank stare, seemingly allowing me time to absorb the impact of her words. She meant business this time.

After shuffling my feet, making sure I had my thoughts organized, with a soft and thoughtful voice, I pleaded, "Please give me a little more time with this thing. You know I'm a fighter and not one to give up. I can do this. Just give me a little more time to figure out how. Mom, I don't think Green Oaks can add anything new to all the good counseling I've received from almost everyone in the whole world. Just please continue to have faith in me, and I'll work this thing out." Pretty good line, I thought, holding back tears as I said words not really on my mind.

What I really wanted to say was: I wish everyone would just leave me alone, allowing me to disappear into the clouds until this was over. I am so tired of all this. Mom put her arms around me with a long and loving embrace. There was no more conversation about Green Oaks.

Struggling with my faith still felt like an uphill battle. I couldn't even repeat the Lord's name under my breath anymore without a feeling of separation from God. Hiding from God out of shame was just one issue, but trusting God to help me fix my pain seemed to be an even greater task. The Bible promises Jesus will never "leave you or forsake you," but I didn't *feel* God. Instead, I felt spiritually empty. All the professional help and medications weren't working as well as everyone hoped. *Was the mass of my inner pain irredeemable?*

The Passion of the Christ, the movie, came out in theaters during the spring of 2004. Mom often expressed her concern about my lack of interest in Christian related activities and questioned me as to why I wasn't praying or talking about Jesus in our household. She saw *The Passion of the Christ,* and said it would help me get to know Jesus in a different light.

She told me about the movie and mentioned it aroused the interest of many private schools and church youth groups. My school followed the religious trend and planned to take my class to see it on a school day in March, in place of our once-a-week chapel session. I had mixed feelings—a movie field trip was a perfect excuse to skip school, but I didn't want to ride the bus or sit with my classmates at the theater.

Later that same evening, after retiring to my room, I grabbed a textbook from the nightstand and held it in a reading position while propped up in bed with pillows. After a few minutes of reading, Mom knocked on my door and asked, with her usual motherly tone of voice, if we could talk some more. "How are you doing?" she asked.

"Just fine—thought maybe I should catch up on some schoolwork."

Mom eased into a sitting position on my bedside, smiled, and didn't waste a minute telling me about a "great idea" on how I could attend *The Passion of the Christ* without having to ride the bus or sit with my classmates during the movie. She got to her feet and moved to sit in a straightbacked chair facing me. "You remember Pam Nigg don't you?" I sat in silence and thought about Pam. She was a friend of Mom's and her laugh could brighten anyone's day. "Of course I remember Pam."

"Well, Pam called me a few minutes ago and I told her how you weren't comfortable going to the movie. It so happens that Pam is just dying to see this movie, and she suggested you go with her in her car and sit together during the movie. What do you think about that?"

I was still fretting and a little pouty from our conversation earlier in the day when Mom insisted I attend this particular movie. Yet, my mood changed instantly and I managed a real smile after hearing her suggestion. It only took a minute for my answer: "I don't want to ride the bus or sit near anyone in my class if I go, so, definitely—yes!"

The teachers were informed that Pam was taking me to the movie in her car, and I was waiting by the school bus, watching my classmates load into the buses, when she arrived.

Before walking into the theater, I pulled the hood of my navy blue, floppy sweater over my head and trudged along beside Pam, wishing I could totally disappear.

As the movie moved along, I slowly became aware of something completely new to my senses and could have jumped straight out of my chair. It was then—right there in the theater that I realized I didn't know Jesus at all, and hadn't really known Him well the past few years. That's why I was so uncomfortable with hearing His name, or asking for His guidance. All those Bible study classes and faithful church attendances, and I never really understood even a fraction of how much God cared for me. I was spiritually oppressed and carried shame I no longer wanted. In all my life I had never seen a movie that affected me so profoundly. At that moment, instead of running from God's love, I wanted to embrace it and feel His goodness seep inside my whole being.

As the movie ended, I felt limp and weak, wondering if I could navigate down the stairs and out the door. Throughout the years of abuse I endured, I lost sight of the fact that God is a loving God. He hated the injustice I suffered more than I did. If I trusted Him, instead of hiding from Him, He would help me. I was sure of it. I was ready to change my life, but I didn't know where to start.

When I saw Mom that evening, I told her I had something important to tell her. After noticing the troubled look on her face, I giggled and assured her the news was *good,* explaining in detail the scenes that had the most effect on me. She seemed to hang on my every word.

Grabbing her hand and holding it tightly, I said, "When I got back to school the Bible teacher prayed with me." Emotionally charged, I proclaimed, "I want to know God in a new way!" She asked me if I really meant what I prayed. Looking in her eyes, I said, "I meant every word." She put her hands over her mouth and squealed with joy. She leaned in and gave me one of the longest hugs I had ever received from her. This time, I hugged her back.

CHAPTER 18

As I arrived home from school a few weeks after spring break, Mom met me at the door. She put her arms around me, allowing, what seemed at the time, an unusually long, loving embrace. After depositing my schoolbooks on the dining room table and moving to the kitchen, I saw Dad working on his laptop. He raised his head and said, "Hi, Honey," and that's when I saw his eyes and instantly knew there was more.

"What's wrong, Dad?" I asked.

"I just received a call from the Denton County District Attorney's office," he stated. "Mark was granted another continuance. It seems he fired his attorney, and he's being allowed another continuance to find someone else to represent him, but don't worry," he added, "It's going to happen. We just have to be patient and remember that the good Lord is on our side."

I had nothing to say, thinking about all those days and weeks spent on preparing to finally say what happened in court.

My CACDC counselor for court preparation couldn't disguise her own disappointment, but she didn't act surprised. "I see this happen frequently," she said. "It's hard for the best of our professionals to get inside the heads of these perpetrators, but

I am willing to bet he's trying to buy time." She went on to say perpetrators are notorious for dragging out the court process as long as they can.

Each day I continued to grow closer to Mom's friend, Pam, who gave me a ride to see *Passion of the Christ*. I called her Pammy. She had short brown hair and a heart the size of Texas. Her big brown eyes lit up each time she laughed. Pammy was a human version of a fantasy fairy godmother to me, always dressed in her favorite color, purple, and ready to answer my call. However, I was still struggling with accepting love from anyone outside my immediate family. The walls I built around myself over the years to protect me emotionally had grown high—so high that they imprisoned me.

Mom sensed my mistrust and suspicions of close friends and others, so it didn't surprise me when she sat me down one night and offered a simple explanation: "Honey, it's like removing the layers of an onion. You can't expect to regain trust in people overnight. It takes time." Mom's solution made perfect sense. But what no one understood is trusting in others was just one small part of my unsteady life.

Pammy continually offered her friendship and encouragement. Many times, when I felt the most need, I went to her house and visited for various periods of time. She was a role model for me. One day she presented me with a new Bible study book and suggested we do a study together. Each day we completed a new lesson. We took turns reading to each other. She was so loving and reassuring, saying I was like the daughter she never had. We often enjoyed our Bible study in Pammy's backyard sipping tea and snacking on cheese and crackers either in her pool or while being soothed by warm, forceful jets in her large hot tub.

Pammy's time, thoughtfulness, and optimism touched my heart. One day, she came up with an idea to help me get through each day at school. She called it my "present drawer." She filled the drawer with various articles of jewelry so that the whole drawer sparkled. If I attended all my classes and turned in my assignments on time I could choose a gift from the present drawer.

At school, I continued to be isolated from almost all social interactions. Not knowing how to deal with a "victim," friends and other students hurried by me with their head and eyes toward the floor. No one—my parents, counselors or teachers—could even imagine what was going on inside my head. Traumatized is not a strong enough word to explain my mental state.

My algebra teacher, Mr. Kinney, was still patiently tutoring me during my lunch hour every day. Intense focus in tutoring didn't allow me time to think about my life and served as a distraction from my everyday anxieties. The tutoring sessions were instrumental in submitting my homework on time, yet, if I didn't continue to raise my overall grade, summer school was the ultimatum. My final paper test would determine summer school.

I was so desperate that I brought Mr. Kinney a large apple pie two weeks before finals. He chuckled and thanked me, "How did you know apple pie was my favorite?"

"I don't know, just a lucky guess," I said. My heart was racing. I didn't know where to take the conversation from there. I didn't have a plan, but needed to express my desperation to pass algebra and prayed he had a magic formula to get me through the class.

Mr. Kinney leaned forward in his desk chair, pencil in one hand, occasionally tapping the eraser on the desktop while I unfolded my story: "I feel terrible about flunking algebra, Mr. Kinney, and it's not your fault. Everyone knows you're a good teacher. But, I want you to know I'm trying really hard. . . ." Half-way through my plea Mr. Kinney interjected. He said he knew something about what was happening in my life, but " . . . in my class you either pass or you don't pass." Despite my plea, he was willing to continue tutoring as long as I continued, "putting forth the required effort."

I responded with an enthusiastic, "Thank you so much, Mr. Kinney. I won't disappoint you. Promise!"

Test day came and guess who was the last one to submit her test paper? Outside the classroom I paced the hallways and impatiently leaned against the wall near the door waiting for test results. Finally, the door opened and Mr. Kinney told me to "Come on in" and motioned for me to sit down. He pushed the test paper toward me and leaned back in his chair as I gasped at a maze of red marks while desperately searching for a grade. There was none.

Massive red marks meant one thing—*Hello summer school.* I hung my head and continued to stare at the paper when he straightened up in his chair and started to talk, with a more pleasant expression on his face this time. "It's interesting," he stated. "You got the bonus question right. Only five other students in the class got it. The extra points bring your grade up to 70. Congratulations, you passed the class."

"I passed?" I was stunned.

Driving home after school, my heart swelled with a sense of achievement, thinking about how excited Mom and Dad would be when I told them the news. Dad wasn't home, but I wasn't disappointed with Mom's reaction. "Oh, . . . my gosh," Mom squealed. "Praise Jesus! Oh, thank God!" We celebrated by holding hands and jumping up and down, with Lauren looking on with a puzzled expression.

When our celebration finally died down a few decibels, Lauren raised her voice up to be heard. "Mom, Jenna got a C in math. How come you don't get excited about my grades like that? She made a C! You're always telling me to work harder to make all A's!"

Mom let out a little chuckle. "Well, I never knew I would rejoice over any of my kids making a C, but Jenna was failing."

"Mom, I don't understand." Lauren puckered her lips.

"Well, just remember, I still expect you to get an A on most of your work, Lauren. This grade was just an exception."

Several weeks before the end of my junior year in high school, Mom started checking on other schools where I would likely be unknown and accepted on my own merits. She reasoned that my extreme absentee record could not continue if I expected to graduate as a senior next year with my class.

Mom sat me down before the end of school for what she referred to as a "serious" talk. After she was sure I understood the seriousness of this past year's performance and the slight chances that anything would improve, she felt safe in dropping the big one. "There are several schools where you would be eligible to transfer," she said.

I interrupted her, "Mom, I have gone to this school since the second grade. It's all I know."

"I know, but just hear me out," she started. "You know that your Uncle Pat and Aunt Roberta have offered you a chance to finish your senior year in Colorado Springs. What do you think about that?"

"I don't know, Mom. But it's a nice gesture by them."

"OK, there's something else I want you to consider. There are alternative schools close enough that you could live at home and finish your senior year."

I caught my breath. "Mom! I know what alternative schools are! That's where the schools send pregnant teens, juvenile delinquents, and outcasts. Which category fits me?"

Mom chuckled at my assessment of alternative schools, but she wasn't through talking. "There are many good things about these schools that public and private schools don't offer, which is why some parents choose to send their kids there."

I withered at the thought that Mom would even consider sending me to an alternative school and wanted this discussion to end. So, I said what I thought would be my last and final words on the subject: "Mom, let's please end this talk about me graduating at an alternative school. What will I tell people the rest of my life when they ask where I went to high school?"

Mom smiled. "OK, but promise me you will at least visit one of these schools with me before shutting your mind down on the possibility."

Nodding my head to agree, I let out a deep sigh and said, "I promise. And you can finish telling me about all the other good things these schools offer."

"You'll have two choices for attending class. You can choose morning classes or afternoon classes. You're allowed to work at your own pace, even to the point of graduating early—I mean like, even in one semester if you work hard enough. That's about all I know at the moment. But I have a feeling we will get a real education during our visit to one, which I will arrange as soon as possible."

Less shunning, more free time, and the opportunity to graduate early didn't seem too bad when I thought about it, but with so many other things weighing heavily on my mind, the last thing I wanted was to make a big decision.

Willow Bend Academy was the first alternative school Mom chose to visit. It was located in Plano, Texas, about twenty minutes driving time from our house. At least the name "Willow Bend" seemed friendly. Willow Bend Shopping Mall was one of the nicest places to shop in the area, but I had never seen a school near the place. "Are we lost?" My eyes centered on a Christian bookstore to the right of our parking space, and it flashed through my mind that this must be the place Mom bought a whole library of Christian books for me to read.

"No, Honey," Mom let out a little laugh. "We're here. Look at the brick building right in front of you, Willow Bend Academy."

Confused, I thought, *How, could a school be located in the middle of a huge shopping complex?*

After explaining to the school receptionist the purpose of our visit, we were asked to wait while she contacted a school representative to show us around. They were expecting us.

The first thing I noticed was the layout. There were no classrooms. Students had their own cubicle. The whole school looked like a business office and was unusually quiet. We walked over to the "testing center," a long table in the back corner of the room where students were tested at different times. After we observed the testing center we walked down each cubicle row, which was distributed according to grade level. The private cubicle spaces appealed to me. *If I worked in a cubicle I could focus more on getting work done and maybe graduate early.*

As we strolled around the facility, students seemed involved in what they were doing and never turned away from their work to watch our movements. Everything about this school was different, the building, the cubicles, the classroom instruction, the testing methods, and the homework.

When the tour ended, I felt I had enough information to help me decide where to spend my senior year. If I chose the alternative school, there were no extracurricular activities to participate in, and I couldn't start over socially even if I chose to do so. They didn't have any dances, sports teams, or clubs. In fact, both of my school options socially deprived me of a typical fun senior year. Transferring meant I wouldn't graduate with classmates I'd known since second grade. Thinking about all this, I couldn't see a real choice—I couldn't possibly bear another year being treated as a blamed victim.

On the drive home Mom asked me for my thoughts about the school. As I looked out the window I said, "I don't want to visit any more alternative schools. Willow Bend Academy seems different but doable. *If* I transfer, Willow Bend is where I'll go."

That same day, I told Mom my decision, and it wasn't without a few tears. I would transfer to Willow Bend Academy to complete my senior year of high school.

Jake Russell and I rarely talked after his father was arrested. I told myself I understood what he was going through. It wasn't just that he was torn between a friend and his father, Mr. Russell had disgraced himself throughout the whole community. How could Jake look anyone straight in the face? In our few short conversations, I tried to reassure him that I understood. However, I questioned my own words. How could I really understand how deeply devastated Jake must be? I despised his father for what he did to all of us, but would I feel that same way if it were my own father? Jake and I both accepted the inevitable—we couldn't turn back the clock. Nothing would ever be the same with us.

As the trial date loomed closer, my family and the remaining members of the Russell family grew further apart. Not long after Mr. Russell's arrest, Stephanie related to me and the rest of my family that she had a conversation with Mr. Russell's daughter, Jackie. Stephanie assured Jackie that our family supported her and her mother in this ordeal. Stephanie wanted her to know we were not blaming her, Jake, or Grace for Mr. Russell's actions. Sometime during the conversation, Stephanie said Jackie became upset, saying "Who is going to walk me down the aisle when I get married?" Later, Dad told Stephanie to tell Jackie he would walk her down the aisle.

At one point after Mr. Russell's arrest, Grace told Mom she could no longer maintain their friendship. It was too hard on her, and she needed to walk alongside her husband. She knew he was wrong, but she was going to support him in the courtroom. Grace later filed for divorce.

Overall, each of us in my family communicated openly our support for everyone in the Russell family (of course, with the exception of Mr. Russell). However, despite our best efforts to get along, we could not maintain those relationships for the long term.

PURE IN HEART

Grace still cared for her soon to be ex-husband. Jackie and Jake still loved their father. Although Mr. Russell moved out of their home, he maintained contact with his family. I had to keep reminding myself that I was not to blame. Mr. Russell not only stole my innocence, he was solely responsible for practically destroying two families.

In addition to regular one-on-one counseling sessions at the CACDC, I also continued to attend court preparation sessions. After one of my court preparation sessions, I questioned whether the court counseling was worth my time and effort because in my present state of mind I struggled to remember information considered important when on the stand.

About a week before the trial, I was standing in the kitchen cooking dinner with Mom when the phone rang and Dad took the call in the living room. Dad shot into the kitchen with a distressed look on his face. "He rescheduled again," were his first words.

"No! I don't believe it," Mom replied, slowly, with emphasis on each word.

One of my counselors informed me it might happen again, and after previous disappointments, I expected it. So, I wasn't going to jump up and down, yell, and make a scene to demonstrate my true feelings.

Mr. Russell's rescheduling tested what little faith I had during the summer months, but I hoped that by exercising my faith it would grow, allowing me the confidence needed to persist. I didn't always *feel* as though I had any faith, especially in the judicial system. Help in this endeavor came from the overwhelming support I found at the CACDC group counseling where I learned that other girls my age struggled in some of the same areas. While in group counseling sessions, I didn't feel alone in my battle to keep fighting the good fight of faith.

My parents continued to attend the CACDC family counseling where they received support from other parents going through the same thing. We all prepared in our own ways for the challenge before us.

Shortly before his last day of the rescheduled court date, Mr. Russell asked the judge for more time to hire a new lawyer to put his case together. Thankfully the judge refused on grounds that Mr. Russell was previously granted sufficient time to hire someone to represent him. The case would be heard at the next scheduled time with, or without, his counsel.

"It's about over," people close to me kept repeating in my ear. But what they didn't understand was it would only be over for Mr. Russell. No matter what the jury verdict, I would come in second. It wouldn't be over for me.

CHAPTER 19

Monday morning, the last week in August 2004, was a day I had anguished over, while at the same time looked forward to, for nearly three months. It was the day set for my escape from the reality of silent rejection and self-condemnation—my first day in a new school since second grade.

The day was greeted with both wonderment and terror, but neither of these emotions were voiced to Mom or Dad. They had to prepare for their own everyday work problems—Mom with a roomful of rowdy school kids, and Dad facing the possibility of replacing an employee who failed to show up for work. I wanted them to believe I was looking forward to this new experience in a strange school—*just another first day of school, as always.* Much later I would look back on this scene and wonder just how much of my false bravado they bought.

The last thing I wanted was to be recognized as the new kid in school. I wanted to just blend in. I must have changed outfits six or seven times before finally deciding upon jeans and a plain black T-shirt.

Shortly after entering the door of Willow Bend Academy, a female person of authority directed me to an assembly room for first year students. Something about her warm countenance and long flowing skirt helped to calm me. I was to learn later that this same person would be one of my instructors.

We were allowed to introduce ourselves before being assigned a teacher for specific subjects. Classes were divided into two half-day sessions, morning and afternoon. I chose the morning session so I could have my afternoons open to do homework or go to Pammy's house.

It didn't take more than a casual observation of this group to dismiss all my anxieties about standards of dress, or "blending in." Clearly, most acted shy and insecure about their surroundings. I was one of them now, a new alternative student just waiting for a chance to quietly escape into my separate little cubicle.

Surprise and panic emerged as I read through my first lesson plans programmed to allow students to learn on an individual basis. At first it was a lonely feeling, enclosed in my little cubicle, but the quiet time and added focus actually increased my concentration and learning ability. It wasn't long before I relaxed with the reality of working through my problems alone, getting right down to why I was here, accepting my individuality, and viewing my work as something more like what it really was, a single effort.

I was astonished at how quickly time passed. Stepping out on the street, shortly past noon, I felt heady and celebratory, finishing a full day of schoolwork in four hours. I was free.

As one of only a few seniors, I reasoned that the other seniors were there because something tragic happened in their life to cause a change in schools. I knew this wasn't a fair assumption, but, I had nothing better to go on. We were not pressed to reveal any personal history during the introductions, which was the norm for the school.

My cubicle was near a younger, middle school girl. She introduced herself as Mariella (a name I had never heard before) that first day of school. She was a tall, thin, rather attractive, dark-skinned little girl who spoke perfect English. Mariella kept mostly to herself, even though she sat in the adjoining cubicle. I noticed her only when she walked to or from her cubicle, books held to her thin body with both hands and eyes glued to the floor. She favored all black clothing and seldom spoke more than two words to anyone. As time went on, I saw her catching glances at me with an inquiring expression. Our greetings became friendlier on a daily basis and once I even caught her wearing a thin smile.

Just before noon one day I was bent over my desk, finishing up a lesson, when I had the sensation someone was staring at me from behind my chair. I slowly turned around to see Mariella standing perfectly still, one hand holding two books to her chest and the other outstretched toward me, holding a single sheet of paper. "I wrote you a note," she whispered. Her next words were spoken so softly as to be barely audible. "Please don't tell anyone."

We made eye contact as she handed me the single piece of paper. I laid the sheet of paper on my lap while still keeping eye contact. "Don't worry," I replied. "I have something to tell you, too, but not right now."

I turned back to my desk, unfolded the paper, and started to read as soft footsteps faded away. She explained some of the pain she was suffering through, and she was using self-harm to cope with some things.

I wanted to help her somehow but didn't know what to do.

Get up and run as fast as you can and give the note to the principal at this school, I told myself over and over. But, I couldn't do it. No matter what, I couldn't betray her trust.

So, I decided to write her a secret note in return and thanked her for sharing personal information with me. I begged her to tell a person of trust who could help her right away and, that if she couldn't tell, I would tell for her. I also explained that I was going through something similar and was in the process of healing, adding that I would be there for her if she needed someone—that I would be praying for her.

A few days later, she motioned me aside in a hallway while I was navigating my way around students to reach my cubicle. She caught my arm, nudged me closer, and whispered close to my ear, "I thought about what you said in your note. And I am ready to tell."

She wasn't smiling, but I could sense a lift in her voice, maybe a small ray of hope finally shining through. I gave her a hug and told her how proud I was of her. She told me she planned to tell one of the teachers later that day.

"Do you need me to go with you?" I asked.

"Thank you, but no. I think I can finally do this by myself," she said.

I told her she was a brave soul for doing it alone. That was the last time we discussed the situation. Until this day she has always had a part in my evening prayers, but I never learned if anyone actually followed through with her outcry for the help she so desperately needed.

On the drive home the last day of school, I thought of Mariella again. *Who was she? Was she an orphan? Living in a homeless environment, or living in a home with one or more parents addicted to drugs?*

In the days and months ahead, I couldn't push Mariella out of my thoughts. To me, we were connected and represented so many abused children in the world, and I just couldn't stop thinking about it, and silently asking myself questions: *What are schools doing to help abused children tell? How many more abused children (both boys and girls) are out there feeling hopeless, silently begging for attention and help?* I couldn't answer any of my own questions. But I knew I would never forget this little girl and that my list of questions would get longer.

As time progressed I was amazed at how relaxed and satisfied I was at working alone in a quiet environment. My time was singularly devoted to getting my work done. I quickly blazed through assignments, quizzes, and tests. As the days passed, I felt better and better about my choice to switch schools, and I thanked God every day for helping me make that crucial decision.

"I have good news for you, Jenna," announced my teacher, as she patted me on the back, "You are already over halfway done with the school year. If you keep up this pace, you can graduate in just a few months." I couldn't believe my ears.

"I really hope so," I said. Then she showed me the work I needed to complete to make it happen. I was almost done and couldn't wait to tell Mom and Dad.

Mom had news to tell me, too. I wanted to hear her news first. "We have our final date for the trial. It's November eighth."

"That's only a couple months away!" I gasped. Now I had a new goal—to finish school before the trial. I didn't know how I was going to work faster, but I was determined to try. Going through finals at the same time as the trial sounded like sheer torture. At least I had a deadline now, and I was fixed on finishing my senior year.

After school each day I started taking assignments home and did a full day's work instead of half a day.

As the September weeks passed, I kept my energy focused on schoolwork. The day finally arrived when it was time to take final exams, and I was on edge to say the least. I explained my dilemma to my teacher, and she promised to grade my papers first to allow me extra time to retest "if necessary."

I hooked my feet around the chair legs and waited impatiently for her to finish grading my last test. When finished, she walked out of the teacher's office and smoothed down her long skirt. Then, she gave me a quick hug and said, "Congratulations on your exam. You're going to graduate."

"Really, that's it? I'm finished?" I shrieked.

"Yes, you are," she clarified. "All that's left is to submit the paper work and wait for your diploma in the mail. I'm so proud of you." By October 2004 the required coursework for my senior year of high school was completed.

With school finished, my new focus was on the upcoming trial. Although I felt confident with my counseling, I was terrified to face Mr. Russell in the courtroom and voiced this fear to one of my female court preparation counselors. She looked at me as if her next words should be remembered forever: "Jenna, I want you to start thinking of this man for what he is—your *opponent*.

He no longer has any power over you. He knows there's a real possibility he could be facing many years behind bars, and if he is like all the others I've dealt with, he will be a hundred times more scared in the courtroom than you could be in your wildest dreams."

She paused but did not change her expression. "You must go into that courtroom with a fighting spirit, knowing there is a battle to be fought and won. Again, you are no longer a victim. *You* are his opponent."

She finished and sat back in her chair with a wide smile. "We've covered a lot of things today. There's so much more for us to discuss before the trial, but I believe you have enough to take home with you for one day."

Even with all of my pretrial counseling, taking the witness stand never felt like an easy task. The details of my abuse were ugly, and I dreaded having to actually say them out loud for all in the courtroom to hear. I didn't want my family and friends to know *everything*. Even though my counselor told me several times, "It's not your fault," I still struggled with feeling embarrassed. All the pieces were coming together in one of the biggest moments of my life.

CHAPTER 20

A couple of weeks before our scheduled November 8, 2004, court appearance, Mom came into my bedroom fired up about something and said, "Jenna, I just got off the phone with Pammy. She wants to make a white awareness ribbon for you to wear when you testify. Across the face of the ribbon it would read, *Pure In Heart* in silver letters." My eyes lit up, and then they filled with tears. "I love that idea," I said.

Mom explained that the white ribbon was a symbol of my innocence and purity. It was a visual reminder that the acts committed against me didn't taint the purity of who I really am.

She continued, "That's not all. Pammy and I thought it would be a great idea if everyone else who supports us wears the ribbon as well. We hope the visual of the ribbon will help give you strength to testify on the witness stand."

At that moment I was a breath away from feeling pure all over. I could feel my chest rise and fall, picturing all those white ribbons on our side of the courtroom and trying to get into the supporters' minds and emotions. *Would they still think me "pure" after what I had to say on the stand about my purity?*

I wanted to call Pammy right then and tell her how much I

love her for everything she's done for me—especially the ribbons, but all I could do at the moment was hug Mom and finish my cry.

A few days before we were to make the long awaited car drive to the Denton County courthouse, a phone call came from lead State Prosecutor Jeff Fleming. He informed us that Mark Russell pleaded guilty, but with "ulterior" motives. This meant we didn't have to go through the guilty or innocent part of the trial. Now we only had the trial on punishment. Jeff also explained that in the trial on punishment, some evidence admitted into a guilt or innocent trial is not allowed. It was to Mark's advantage to plead guilty and not have some of the damaging evidence against him presented. Mark also chose the option allowing a jury to rule upon his sentence.

After the phone call, it took me awhile to understand the implications of pleading guilty with *ulterior motives*. All I firmly understood was that Mr. Russell had pleaded guilty and that was enough to cause a small celebration in our household, and a very personal satisfaction that I had persevered.

I was restless the night before our trial date. Even though my eyes were closed, my mind raced. *What if the jury doesn't believe me or doesn't think he should be punished?* As my anxiety rose to a new height, I turned to prayer.

This time I felt compelled to pray, not just for myself, but also for everyone, including Mr. Russell. I recalled the verse in the Bible that urged us to pray for our enemies. *But I tell you: Love your enemies and pray for those who persecute you.* I had avoided this verse until now. *How could I pray for him after what he did? Even worse, how could I wish him blessing?*

But I knew I had to forgive. As long as I held on to unforgiveness and bitterness I was carrying my abuser and his impact on my life into each and every day. So I hoped that if I prayed, then maybe my emotions would catch up. My desire was to show God that I was *trying* to forgive.

> *Lord, please help me to say what I need to say when I need to say it. Be with my family as they are going through this, too. Also, please be with the Russell family. You say to pray for those who persecute me, and so I'm trying. Forgive me if it's not sincere and help my emotions to follow my words. Please help Mr. Russell in all the ways you know he needs help—bless him. And I am praying for all those who will persecute me at the trial tomorrow and afterward. I pray that no person or thing will stand in the way of my relationship with you. Your will be done, Lord; whatever that is, I trust it.*

Forgiveness I have learned is not for the faint at heart. I said the prayer, but I felt guilty because my heart was not fully into the forgiveness mode. *How could I possibly be honest with myself about asking God to bestow his blessings upon a man who had stolen my innocence and caused so much heartache for so many other people?*

When my feet hit the floor on the morning of November eighth, I knew right away I was not ready for what was to come. Still woozy from lack of sleep, I had a weak stomach. Getting more sleep wasn't possible because we had to arrive at the courthouse early.

When I walked downstairs, the smell of bacon was in the air. My Grandma, Ceci Quinn, from El Paso, Texas, was making breakfast, but I didn't have much of an appetite.

Several family members who came into town from miles away to sit in the courtroom and show their support were present, and after breakfast we all stood around the table, held hands, and listened to separate prayers from Mom and Dad, each thanking God for our case to be heard by a jury.

Outside the courthouse I noticed some familiar bikes lined up in the parking lot. B.A.C.A. was there in full biker dress—du-rags, gloves, black B.A.C.A. vests, and boots. Looking stern and standing out, they greeted us with hugs, each pledging their support.

After we rushed through the security screening, my mouth was dry and I asked for some water. A member of B.A.C.A. scurried to get water, but there was no time to wait. We had to find the two Denton County prosecutors, Jeff Fleming and Debra Bender, as well as Beverly Bailey, a licensed professional counselor assigned to my case as a Child Victim Intervention Specialist.

Attorney Debra Bender was the real deal in a two-piece skirt suit. She was slender with shinning black hair, fine facial features, and an easy smile. You could perceive in her sparkling, intelligent eyes and demeanor—she was there to win. She was how I pictured myself when grown.

Beverly Bailey was all business in a two-piece, dark blue suit. She was in her thirties, medium height with a natural, outdoorsy complexion and short, close-cropped hair. Her kindly, attractive face with warm brown eyes and arresting smile generated a look about her that made her stand out in public. Talking with her through this tough time was soothing.

I visited with my prosecution team at least twice before our court appearance, always when Dad or Mom was nearby or present. Now I was getting a closer look at each one, together and separately, and I was beginning to feel like they were my second family—protective and just for me. I considered Attorney Jeff Fleming my bodyguard while we were in the courthouse. He was always there for me, and I felt safe—on the stand and when I was near him.

It was easy to feel that way. Attorney Fleming was in his mid-thirties, standing about six-feet, stout and rugged, with a fierce demeanor. However, his approach to our team defied his intimidating appearance. He had some of Dad's teddy bear gentleness about him.

As we walked farther into the courthouse, Beverly and I spotted each other at the same time. "I need some water," was the first thing I said to her. She escorted us down a hallway and stopped at a water fountain located just outside the witness room where people scheduled to testify against Mr. Russell stayed during the trial.

The only time I was allowed into the courtroom was when I gave my own testimony. Those in the gallery (seating for public and/or press), the jurors, counselors, and Mr. Russell were the only people allowed to see the entire trial.

Beverly told us to leave our personal belongings in the witness room until we returned from a prosecution team briefing. We followed her down another hallway and into a private room where we met with the Denton County prosecutors, Jeff and Debra.

"How are you this morning?" Attorney Fleming asked.

"I really don't want to see Mr. Russell," I said.

"You're going to be just fine. Don't worry about him." Then the prosecutors briefed us on what to expect for the day.

I started to feel better as we walked back to the witness room, until we turned a corner and almost bumped into Mr. Russell and James Caldwell, his defense attorney. I froze, feeling as if the wind had been knocked out of me. He was glaring at me. I could feel his hatred in every nerve of my body as a wave of terror hit me. It felt as though he could see right through me. For those few seconds, it felt like we were the only two people around. Debra saw my reaction, took my arm, and hastily pulled me back. "Come this way," she said.

As we waited in the witness room, I was still feeling his presence and seeing the scowl on his face as the room got smaller and smaller. I had to get out of there, if only for a few minutes. "I need a restroom break," I whispered to Beverly. She agreed it was a good idea for both of us. She escorted me to the restroom, along with two B.A.C.A. members waiting in the hall.

My frustration grew and I wanted to know, word for word, how the defense attorney presented the case. I had suffered for so long, and, now that my hidden horrors were being exposed into the light, I felt deprived and cheated because I couldn't hear what was said.

Years later, doing research for this book, the burning desire was still there to know what was said. I found my answers in the court transcript, and portions of the transcript are used below.

Attorney Jeff Fleming gave the first opening statement:

"Ladies and gentlemen of the jury, I anticipate that the evidence in this case will show that the kind of people who commit indecency with a child or sexual assault of a child don't wear certain uniforms so that they can be identified. Child molesters don't carry signs that say, 'Beware. Keep Your Children Away From Me. I'm Dangerous.' But the evidence will show that they are in our own back yards. They are invited into our homes. They are members of our church. They are even in our schools. The evidence in this case will show that this defendant and his entire family were very good friends with the victim's family. . . .

"Jenna's Dad is Greg. This defendant and Greg Quinn were best friends, did things together all the time. These families celebrated birthdays together. These families celebrated holidays together. These families went on vacations together. They were close, very close. The evidence will also show that not only was he a family friend and had access to her, this defendant helped coach her basketball team at the school, that he was one of her coaches, one of the authority figures who are supposed to be teaching her, molding her, not molesting her. . . .

"The evidence will show that he, that he is a sexual predator, and she was the prey. And I anticipate at the end of the trial I'm going to stand right up here in front of you, and I'm going to ask you to go back there and put him in prison for a long time, because that's what he deserves."

After opening statements the judge asked for the first witness from the state.

Attorney Fleming stated my name, "Jenna Quinn."

As I was summoned, I took a deep breath, feeling frightened and shaky as I stepped up to the stand. The bailiff held a Bible in front of me to place my hand on and repeat what any TV viewer can repeat by memory.

"I swear to tell the truth . . . so help me God."

Then the judge asked me to be seated.

My hands started to shake. I didn't know what to do with

them. I placed them under my legs, then pulled them out and placed them on my lap and put pressure on them, which helped to keep them still.

Mr. Russell sat only a few feet away from the stand with his eyes fixed on me. I avoided eye contact with him as much as I could. When I sat down, I took a quick glance at the people in the gallery, to get an eyeball overview of who was sitting where. What I saw was reassuring. So many friends and family came from out of town to be there for me, and they wore the *Pure In Heart* white ribbons. I glanced at the jury to my right, then quickly away.

Mr. Russell was five feet away, directly to my left, in plain sight. I could see his every gesture and hear his every sniffle and snuffle.

Attorney Fleming walked toward me to start with questions.

He began with simple questions—my name, age, and the school I attended. I answered these questions as confidently as possible. Talking about school allowed him to ask me about extracurricular activities, like basketball. Then he shifted topics and asked me if I knew the defendant. I replied that I did in fact know the defendant.

Attorney Fleming asked me to talk about when I first met Mr. Russell and the relationship between the two families. I talked about how Mr. Russell played several roles in my life and in my family's life. I explained that he was the father of two of my closest friends growing up, Jake and Jackie.

Then the questions got more specific. "Describe for the jury the point when you noticed that your relationship with Mr. Russell was beginning to change. What did he do?" I took a deep breath and described as quickly as I could all the sexual things he said to me throughout the years.

As I nervously rambled on, the prosecutor said, "Jenna let me stop you right there." He wanted me to describe from the beginning when it all started, at a slower pace. He wanted to know where Mr. Russell and I were when he started talking about sexual things and he wanted the conversations in detail.

I had a brave face until then.

Thinking back about the first inappropriate situation was overwhelming. I could feel my cheeks getting wet. He briefly waited for me to gain my composure. "Do you need a second?"

I choked up. "That's fine. Take your time," he said.

Then the judge asked, "You need a break? You want to take a break?" I nodded yes. As tears filled my eyes I prayed, *Lord please help me through this.*

The court recessed for fifteen minutes in order for me to get myself together. Still crying, I darted as quickly as I could back to the witness room where Mom, Dad, and Stephanie waited. They comforted me and encouraged me to stay strong and finish my testimony. I didn't expect to get emotional so soon. After hugs, kisses, and lots of water, I was as ready as I could be to get back on the stand.

Attorney Bender came to get me after my fifteen-minute break. When I was on the stand again, Attorney Fleming repeated the question. This time I was composed. I talked about the several car rides home and the sexual comments that were made.

After explaining how Mr. Russell often asked me sexual questions and told me all about his sexual encounters before and after marriage, the prosecutor asked a more personal question. "Do you recall the first time he advanced from speaking about sex to touching you?"

I fought back tears again and said, "Uh-huh." He asked me to explain further.

I elaborated on the first time, and all the other times Mr. Russell sexually assaulted me. As I gave details Mr. Russell sank farther and farther into his seat with every passing minute. At one point, out of the corner of my eye, I saw Grandma leave the room, wiping her eyes with a tissue. Other family members followed her lead. I was relieved when they left. What I had to say was only important to the judge and jury.

After going into detail about the assaults, I was asked how I coped with the pain and why I was afraid to tell. I talked about my insomnia, cutting, depression, and anxiety. I did my best to describe how every area of my life was affected by the trauma and how I went from receiving basketball awards to sitting on the bench; from making good grades to failing; and from being socially involved in extracurricular activities to missing many days of school my junior year. I then described how I made my outcry to Stephanie over lunch.

At the end of the prosecutor's examination, he asked, "This person, the defendant you have been referring to the whole time, do you see that person in the courtroom here today?"

I answered with a confident, "Yes."

He asked me to point and describe where that person was in the room. "He's on my left side." I gestured toward Mr. Russell.

Next, I was asked to count down from the table which person he was. "One, two, three, four." I pointed with my right arm stretched out far. "Four."

As I stared Mr. Russell in the eye and pointed at him, I felt *empowered* around him for the first time. He stared back at me and looked like a wolf waiting for the right timing to eat its prey. I looked back at him and kept my finger pointed toward him.

The prosecutor let us stare at each other for what felt like a whole minute and then said, "Your Honor, may the record reflect that the witness has identified the defendant."

Now, without a break, I was confronted with the hardest part of the trial on punishment. Mr. Russell's defense attorney, James Caldwell, slowly crept toward me to cross-examine. He slanted his questions to attack my character, making it seem as though I was the one who sought after Mr. Russell.

Another major point of his questioning was why I didn't tell sooner. He asked, "Why didn't you tell your family so you could put an end to this?"

I told him it was because our families were so close and his son, Jake, is my best friend. "I thought that if his son ever were to find out, it would break his heart." Overwhelmed with sadness, I started to cry again.

In a sarcastic tone, the defense attorney asked, "You were afraid of breaking Jake's heart?" I nodded my head, yes, as I sobbed. Jake was in a gallery pew sitting behind his father's side of the courtroom. It was a sensitive moment. The room was silent, and then Jake started to get emotional. "I see—and then moving on," said the attorney. Even in my emotional state, I could sense Mr. Russell's attorney realized his sarcasm backfired on him.

Defense Attorney Caldwell argued that his client never forced me to do anything. He also tried to attack my character by making me seem promiscuous with boys my age. I felt myself get angrier by the minute. I experienced a range of emotions from deep sadness, guilt, anxiety, and rage. I felt as though I was re-victimized all over again on the stand.

To make matters worse, I was falsely accused of taking pages out of my journal that described how I enjoyed being with Mr. Russell. They were desperate accusations, and my counselor for court preparation at the CACDC mentioned all these things might happen. As I continued to hear lies, I felt my head clouded with anger and frustration.

I did my best not to fall for any "word traps" and gave it all I had. When the cross-examination was completed, I was excused to return to the witness room. Exhausted is not a strong enough word—I was on the stand for three-and-a-half hours.

As I removed myself from the stand and made my way down the aisle separating the two sides of the courtroom, I felt indescribable *joy* and a sense of accomplishment. The acts committed against me were no longer hidden like skeletons deep within a dark cave. The dishonor I had carried was now where it belonged—on Mr. Russell.

As I walked back toward the witness room, the double doors separating the courtroom from the foyer had closed when I raised my arms up in a shout of joyful victory. "Yes!" I whispered loudly. My heart was soaring with joy and relief. I had done it!

The first day of the trial on punishment was over and mine was the only testimony that day. I was mentally and physically exhausted. Since Mom and Dad were in the witness room during my testimony, and we were all sworn to secrecy, the ride home was thankfully quiet.

We all went to bed early that night, which turned out to be a good thing because what happened the next day tested our limits.

CHAPTER 21

November 9, 2004, was the second day of the trial on punishment, and another early morning. Once again the family joined hands and prayed together after breakfast. Finally, when everyone was dressed and ready to go, we loaded into the car.

B.A.C.A. greeted us when we arrived and walked through security. Jeff Fleming, Debra Bender, and Beverly Bailey also welcomed us and expressed their enthusiasm for the day. As we cruised toward the witness room, I carefully scanned the hallways for Mr. Russell to avoid another accidental run in, and focused on my breathing.

Most who were there to support me the first day of the sentencing trial also came on the second day, wearing the white "Pure In Heart" ribbons. The ribbon really stood out against the black B.A.C.A. vests. And it warmed my heart to think about those who supported me after all I had to say about what was done to me.

There was plenty of time for me to sit around and think in the witness room. So again I anxiously waited—waited to find out what the jury believed should happen to someone who stole my innocence.

When all this was over, the transcript allowed me to see what was said. Portions taken from the court transcript are used to describe what happened for the remainder of the trial on punishment.

Mom was called to the witness stand first. She looked forward to this moment. She wanted to be heard. After being sworn in, Attorney Fleming started with simple questions and also asked about the relationship between the two families. Then he asked how the defendant acted toward me. Mom explained that he always had an unusual fascination with me and gave examples.

Next he asked Mom to describe the kind of child I was before the abuse started. She explained that I was a peacemaker, quiet, and always wanted everyone to be happy. After describing my natural personality, he asked about my changes in behavior. She described my insomnia, explained my weight gain, self-loathing, depression, cutting, suicidal ideation, grade failure, social withdrawal, and absences from school.

She spoke about my emergency room visits due to hives, and how the doctors tried to determine a cause. She elaborated on taking me to specialists who could not find a diagnosis, except for stress. Mom also described my post-traumatic stress attacks, saying that if I saw anybody that looked like the perpetrator, my leg would shake, I had trouble breathing, and I would have to leave where I was that moment. She listed places I had post-traumatic attacks and gave an example of one.

Then Mom was cross-examined by the Defense Attorney James Caldwell, who questioned whether or not it was possible that I was in a bad mental state before the sexual assaults. His cross-examination didn't last long.

Mom gave me a big hug when she walked back into the witness room. Judging by her confidence, I could tell she handled herself beautifully. After a ten-minute recess that morning Mr. Russell was the next person to be sworn in and take the stand.

Mr. Russell and his defense attorney made it seem as though my parents were neglectful and permissive and that I had sexual relations with other individuals. This broke the terms of the trial on punishment outlined beforehand—that prior sexual history was not to be mentioned due to a plea of guilty. Upon breaking the order of the court, the judge discharged his bond and took him into custody for the remainder of the trial.

Then the court proceeded with Mr. Russell on the stand. This time, Prosecuting Attorney Jeff Fleming cross-examined Mr. Russell.

(*Throughout Chapter 21 are portions of questions and answers taken from the trial on punishment transcripts.*)

Q. "And that whole time period until Jenna went to the police and you got arrested and got indicted, at no point did you ever apologize to her. Correct?"

A. "No sir, I did not."

The prosecutor later asked.

Q. "At no point during that time did you ever realize that 'my' actions are inappropriate, these are not the things that 'I'm' supposed to do, there is something wrong, and go and seek help, did you?"

A. "I knew that it was wrong, sir."

Q. "Did you seek help?"

A. "No, sir, I did not."

The prosecutor continued with more questions and then asked.

Q. "You feel sorry for what you did?"

A. "Yes, I do. I'm very sorry for what I've done."

Q. "You feel like you betrayed the trust that Greg instilled in you?"

A. "Yes, sir, I do. This has been a very, very difficult situation for me. I've got a tremendous amount of respect for the Quinns. I care a lot about the Quinns. They have been very good people to me. The situation has been one that has absolutely destroyed me. It's destroyed my family."

After more questions and answers the prosecutor continued.

Q. "You've got two daughters, as a matter of fact?"

A. "Yes, sir."

Q. "How would you feel if someone sexually assaulted your daughter?"

A. "I would be upset."

Q. "You would be mad, wouldn't you?

A. "Yes, sir."

Q. "You would want justice?"

A. "Yes, sir."

Q. "You would want that person punished?"

A. "I would want to know everything about the case before I did that. . . . "

Q. "Are you telling me that if someone sexually . . . "

After more questions, the defendant continued to answer.

A. "I would have to know all of the circumstances involved in it."

Q. "What other circumstances?"

A. "Whether or not she was involved, whether or not she was the one misleading him or trying to do that."

Q. "Are you trying to tell this jury that you were manipulated, sexually manipulated by a 14-year-old girl?"

A. "I'm saying that Jenna made herself very much available."

Q. "So this is her fault?"

A. "No, it's not her fault, it's not her fault."

After more questions, then came a rebuttal from Mr. Russell's attorney, James Caldwell.

Q. "Okay. Now, you've obviously admitted and clarified what you did and did not do. How do you feel about the damage you've caused to Jenna Quinn?"

A. "The heartache and pain that I've caused Jenna is something I've been living with ever since. I know that the things that I've done are wrong. I can never imagine the pain that I've caused her. I know that she's going to have a hard time recovering from it. I'm very sorry for everything that I've done to the Quinns, for their family, all the heartache that I've caused them. It absolutely devastates me. . . . As far as I'm concerned, I will never recover from the damage and the hurt that I have given them. It's something that I feel like I have basically let them down. I've let the family down. I have tremendous respect for Greg and for Kellie. Kellie has got just a sweet spirit. Jenna has such a sweet spirit. Greg is a very good man."

After more questions the defense attorney passed the witness, and Attorney Jeff Fleming asked his final questions.

Q. "You knew it was wrong when you did it. Correct?"

A. "Yes, sir."

Q. "But that didn't stop you. Correct?"

A. "No, sir."

Then Jeff Fleming had no further questions, and Mr. Russell left the stand.

Next a forensic psychiatrist took the stand for Defense Attorney Caldwell. He intended to scientifically explain Mr. Russell's dysfunction. The psychiatrist explained that Mr. Russell was a regressed offender and explained that regressed offenders have chosen to cope with stress in inappropriate ways because of life's circumstances. The psychiatrist also explained that Mr. Russell was undergoing considerable marital stress.

Then James Caldwell asked for a clearer diagnosis.

Q. "And what was your diagnosis?"

A. "I would say that he has an anxiety disorder. It's an atypical anxiety disorder. Basically, he feels threatened by various situations and feels a compulsion to cope by proving himself. And so he would become very aggressive in sports. He would push his children. He would push himself very hard. He had to be a kind of a perfectionist person, and he saw himself as a caretaker. Unfortunately, he was feeling that that role was no longer accepted by the people around him. He sought a new avenue of gratification in that way."

Q. "And that avenue was?"

A. "Sexual activity with Jenna."

Q. "Okay. And he pursued that. And did he speak frankly with you about that?"

A. "Yes"

The psychiatrist continued to testify that Mr. Russell was sorry for what he did and that he was actively seeking help. After the psychiatrist left the stand, everyone except Mr. Russell was released for lunch. Since the judge discharged his bond earlier, Mr. Russell was taken into custody for the remainder of the trial.

The second day felt twice as long as the first. After the psychiatrist, Mr. Russell had six more witnesses take the stand testifying for him. These people included a childhood friend, a current acquaintance from work, a friend who was a police officer, a former work acquaintance, and Mr. Russell's two daughters. They all testified that his character was more good than bad. The former police officer said Mr. Russell was probation material.

The work acquaintance mentioned his generosity and gave examples of his charitable donations to people and organizations. Mr. Russell's first daughter, from a previous marriage, explained that he was a wonderful father and a perfect example of what a father should be. Both daughters also begged for a probation sentencing.

Then the last person called to the witness stand for the day was Dad. I gave Dad a big hug before he left the witness room. Dad was angry, but at the root of his anger was sadness. After he was sworn in the judge asked him to have a seat. As Dad sat down, he wept. The judge called for a fifteen-minute break.

Dad hurried back into the witness room with tears in his eyes. He came straight for me and hugged me with all his might. That's when I lost it, too. After holding me for a while, he regained his composure. "I'm not crying because of you. I just can't believe this moment is here. I have so many emotions I didn't know I would feel today. But I am so proud of you."

After talking with me and holding me, it seemed his spirits were lifted. When he approached the stand a second time, Attorney Jeff Fleming asked questions.

Q. "Mr. Quinn, I realize this is very difficult for you, so I'm going to try to keep it short. Okay?"

A. "Okay."

The prosecutor opened with simple questions and asked him to identity himself.

Q. "How would you characterize, prior to all of this coming up, how would you characterize your relationship with the defendant in this case?"

A. "We, for the last ten years, we did everything together, golfed, movies every weekend, traveled together. . . . When his knee had to be replaced, we were there for him. He was like a brother to me."

Q. "And at any point in time while this was going on, did you have any indication—"

A. "No indication whatsoever."

Q. "Not even the slightest clue?"

A. "Not any clue whatsoever. It was the furthest thing from my mind."

Q. "When you found out what the defendant had done to your daughter, how did that make you feel?"

A. "Ripped my heart out. Ripped my heart out because somebody that I loved so much could do something like that to my child."

Dad elaborated on feeling betrayed since the day he found out.

Q. "Even as you come in here in this courtroom, it's difficult for you?"

A. "Very."

He answered more questions on how the family felt.

Q. "Mr. Quinn, you're aware of the punishment range in this case of probation, two years, all the way up to 20 years?"

A. "Yes, I am."

Q. "In your opinion, what in your heart do you believe is the appropriate punishment?"

A. "The max. Whatever they can give him."

Then the prosecution rested. Next the judge asked the defense attorney if he wanted to cross-examine Dad—he declined.

Dad was the very last person to testify. I was uneasy with the total amount of people who testified on behalf of Mr. Russell, there were eight people, including himself. On my end, it was Mom, Dad, and I. I had to remind myself that prosecutors Fleming and Bender knew what they were doing. For the first time now I sat in the gallery to hear the closing statements made to the jury. Attorney Debra Bender was the first to speak:

"You bring a child into this world as a parent. You watch them grow. You protect them. You teach them. You guide them. As a parent, you always tell them, don't talk to strangers. Don't talk to strangers. . . . We know there is a bad world out there. We see it on the news. We see it on TV. We read about it. . . . That's the face of a child molester right there and these are what these cases look like. There is always a family on this side and a family on that side, and they are both victims, both victims that are—of decisions made by one man. That man right there. . . . Child molesters are charming. They have families. They are in positions of authority. They are coaches. They are teachers . . . this is all about choices that he made, choices that you and I and everybody else can make throughout our lifetime. Choice after choice after choice he had an out. . . . Every choice. And he was fully aware of his consequences. You see, he sat in your chairs. He was on jury duty for this kind of crime, and he came back and told her he was scared. But he kept doing it. He told her don't tell. . . . And out of all the choices that have been made in this whole situation, there is only one choice left. But this time it's out of his hands, and it is in yours. . . . You have a choice to tell Jenna this is not her fault. She did nothing wrong, and she's not a liar. And she was not very available to him. You have a choice to say a lot with your verdict. You see, he told her a long time ago, shh, it's okay. Tell him it's not okay. Thank you."

Next the defense attorney gave his closing statement to the jury where he challenged the jury to consider probation for Mr. Russell.

Attorney Jeff Fleming gave the final statement. "Ladies and gentlemen of the jury. Sexual assault of a child is not a mess-up. . . . Now, it seems to me if the message that you want to send as a jury is that, okay, if you do really good for 50 years or 55, 56 years, then you're allowed to sexually assault a child, you're allowed to commit indecency with a child and we will just—we will give you a free pass, we will give you one free one because you did good before—is that the message you want to send? I don't think so. But that's what they are asking you. That is what they are telling you. . . . You heard exactly what the defense has put on. You heard what they have argued. That's what they are asking you. That's their argument. He's done good all these times before, so you should take it easy on him this time. I don't think that's a message that you want to send, because with your verdict, you send a message. You send a message to this defendant about what you think about what he has done. You send a message to other would-be offenders out there when they are thinking about doing this to some little girl. . . . You send a message to the community because you speak—you are the voice of the community. You're fellow members of the community, and you tell them what it's worth if somebody systematically sexually abuses a child, because you send that message. . . . But let's look at the facts. Did he feel remorseful when this first started, when he started speaking inappropriately about sex to her? No. He didn't feel remorseful. . . . Think about when we find out he felt sorry. He felt sorry after he got caught. . . ."

Then Attorney Fleming read a portion of my journal to the jury to reiterate my feelings at the time.

Then he concluded, "Ladies and gentlemen, I'm going to ask you with your verdict to tell that young lady that she didn't ask for it. This isn't her fault. And you do that by coming up with the most appropriate verdict in this case, and that is to send this defendant to the penitentiary for as long as you possibly can. Thank you."

The jury left the courtroom at 4:53 p.m. to deliberate. At 6:48 p.m., the jury entered the courtroom with the verdict. The judge scheduled a formal sentencing for 9 a.m. the following morning to rule out the verdict.

CHAPTER 22

On the morning of November 10, 2004, there was a more relaxed, cheerful attitude among the many gathered in our house for what I hoped would be our last trip to the Denton County courthouse. It was almost over with—then there would be the long ride home, bearing feelings of subdued victory or total defeat. I was still in the early stages of healing, and no matter what the outcome it wasn't over for me.

Pammy stopped over before breakfast and greeted me with a gift, a new personal journal to document my feelings about the trial. The journal had a picture of an angel on the cover. The cover read "Reflections" across the front.

Arriving at the courthouse early, we found seats close to the front row. "Pammy sit next to me," I whispered. I sat in the gallery for only the second time since the trial had begun, and now I was reflecting on events of the last two days. Sitting straight up on the edge of my seat, silently, taking deep breathes, I felt both pain and joy. To my right, across the aisle, sat Grace with her hands in her lap. They were no longer living together and her divorce from Mr. Russell was final, but she still supported him on his side of the courtroom.

A deep sadness enveloped my whole body. My heart went out for Grace and her two children, Jake and Jackie, and even though Mr. Russell had not expressed any remorse to me or any of my family I had a heartfelt sinking feeling for him, too. *How could he continue to do something he knew would hurt so many people?*

I glanced around to see the many family and friends who surrounded me while my knees bounced up and down with nervous energy. Pammy placed a hand over my knees and whispered, "Write in your new journal, it'll help take your mind off what's to come." Taking her advice helped sooth my nerves, and I wrote in my new journal until I was interrupted by Mr. Russell's entrance into the courtroom.

He entered the courtroom through a different door this time—the door that led to the jail. He looked much older than his fifty-nine years, wearing an orange jump suit, handcuffs, and ankle shackles. He was unshaven and his hair looked like it hadn't seen a comb for a long time. I grabbed Pammy's leg and squeezed it hard, almost jumping out of my seat at the sight of him. He walked with his head down, watching his feet as he shuffled along between two uniformed officers.

We had to wait only a few minutes before the judge entered the courtroom and took his place. He took a few minutes to sort through his papers and get comfortable in his chair. The silence in the courtroom was almost deafening when he started to speak.

Before reading the sentence, he reiterated that the defendant pleaded guilty to two separate indictments, in two different cities. He read the indictments as prepared by the court reporter and explained them separately.

He paused a second to clear his throat, then said, "If the defendant will rise."

My heart leaped, and I locked eyes with Dad.

Offense I, indecency with a child, ten years in prison.
Offense II, indecency with a child, ten years in prison.
Offense III, sexual assault, ten years in prison.
Offense IV, sexual assault, ten years in prison.

Stopping only to clear his throat, the judge started to read the sentencing for the second indictment:

Offense I, indecency with a child, ten years in prison.
Offense II, indecency with a child, ten years in prison.
Offense III, indecency with a child, ten years in prison.

In all, the jury gave him seventy years, with the counts running concurrently. Sentences run concurrently when defendants serve all the sentences at the same time. It would be a ten-year total sentence for each of the two indictments and the judge then *stacked* the two indictments, making it a twenty-year prison term.

Mom and Dad started to tear up, but they contained all but a whimper. Any outburst would be ruled a "contempt of court." My whole body went numb, but my cheeks remained dry. I could hear some murmuring on both sides of the aisle before the judge asked for order in the courtroom and then proceeded to the next part: the victim impact statements.

The victim impact statement is a statement read by either the victims themselves or by a family member of the victim, or victims. It's the chance for the victims to explain how the crimes committed by the defendant impacted their lives and the lives of family members and friends. It's a chance to describe the devastation, heartache and expense caused by the actions of the defendant, without objections from the defendant's lawyer. Since I was emotionally burned out, Mom volunteered to read mine.

The judge motioned for her to take the stand. She stood up quickly and walked purposely toward the stand. As she sat down, she grabbed the microphone and adjusted it toward her so every word she spoke could be heard. She turned her head to the left where she could see Mr. Russell sitting at the defendant's table, looked him in the eye as often as she could, and read the words I prepared for this moment: "I am reading these words on behalf of my daughter, Jenna Quinn."

Words cannot express the pain, horror and terror I have experienced over the years at the hands of Mr. Russell. Every part of me is ruined, my body, my soul and my spirit. I feel broken to the core. Over the years of coping with the abuse, I have forgotten who I am. What it feels like to be normal. I haven't slept two nights in a row since the abuse began. My mother tried everything to help me. I couldn't tell her of my nightmares when I did sleep. How I always hear his voice telling me to "Shh" and that everything was okay.

He didn't care if I cried and said no. He never said he was sorry. How could I sleep knowing his whispers in public places of what he planned to do to me "next time?"

I broke out in large terrible hives several times. They are so painful and took days to heal, even with the medication from the hospital. I was so stressed, yet felt if I told, others would hurt. I thought it was better that one person hurt, than many. I began overeating thinking it would make me ugly and he wouldn't want me.

I avoided dating. I don't trust anyone anymore, especially boys. I felt so helpless and hopeless. I wanted to kill myself many times. I began cutting myself at 14. This was the only way I felt an outlet to the pain and torment he was causing me. It became an emotional release. I am still in so much pain. I feel worthless because I prayed for him to stop and he didn't.

I figured God couldn't love me. I have a hard time believing and trusting anyone now. Everything is so perverted. When people tell me I'm beautiful or special, I feel so much anger and hurt. That is what he used to say to me. I stuffed all my pain inside for so long that trying to cope with it is almost unmanageable for me.

My parents took me to a psychiatrist for help. I have been so depressed, unable to go to school or practice or play on my school basketball team. My psychiatrist said I have Post Traumatic Stress Disorder. I don't want to get out of bed, shower, eat or see my friends. I want to cut and continue to have thoughts of suicide.

I now have panic attacks that I can't seem to help. I can't see men that look like him or I become extremely anxious and fearful. I wish I didn't feel this way. Why did this have to happen to me?

My Dad cries every day and feels helpless. He says he can't bring me justice or heal me. He, my Mom and sisters love me very much. I haven't been able to express my love back for them since he began abusing me. I hate myself and feel so empty. What can I give back?

My parents bought me a promise ring when I turned 16 to help remind me to be a virgin and to remain pure until marriage. They didn't know I was already ruined and violated. They didn't know what I had already seen and experienced. I have worn the ring for them with such guilt and shame. To live in a body that reminds me of memories that I can't forget is tormenting.

Since Mr. Russell claims to be a Christian, was involved in his church, and lived a lie in front of everyone, it has thrown the very nature of God into question for me. Did God think I was not worth protecting?

I am taking Zoloft and Ambilify during the day to help control my depression, panic attacks, need to cut, and suicidal thoughts. I take Lorazepam at night to sleep or Ambien if it was a harder day to live. I am seeing a sexual abuse counselor from the Children's Advocacy Center, a psychiatrist for medication and therapy, and a psychologist for Cognitive Therapy. My parents are going to group therapy at the Children's Advocacy Center and on Zoloft to help with their depression and anxiety over this. My sisters cry a lot and want me to get better. What he has stolen from my family and me makes me so angry. Because he was my father's best friend, it was the ultimate betrayal of trust.

Who can we ever trust again? I will carry the scars on the inside and on the outside for the rest of my life.

Dad prepared something, too. But after my statement, he asked Mom to read his for him. The room was dead silent as she read Dad's statement for Mr. Russell:

How do you declare to be a man of God? How dare you come into my house and talk about God and pray over the food? I was closer to you than my own brother. If anyone were to try and harm you or your family, I would put my life on the line defending you. As much as I hate you right now, I could still not harm your beautiful children. So how could you harm my child if you were supposed to be one of my best friends? Is there any substance to you at all? I pray to God that when your children grow up and have children, they never meet a person like you.

When she finished reading the last word of Dad's statement I would bet the whole room could feel her indignation. Mr. Russell stared at her with what appeared to be disinterest.

When Mom left the stand, the judge asked Mr. Russell if he wanted to address the family. He declined the opportunity. I received no apology. All those "I'm sorry" statements he made earlier were for the jury's ears only. I felt deeply hurt, again. I wanted Mr. Russell to look me in the eyes with true repentance and say those two little words that meant so much to me. I felt foolish for even hoping to get an apology. Today, more than ever, there was a certain coldness and arrogance about him. *Maybe one day he will apologize.*

The room felt tense as the judge waited for Mr. Russell to change his mind and address the family. The image of Mr. Russell sitting in handcuffs in an orange jump suit in the courtroom caused my mind to race in so many different directions during that uncomfortable silence. Anxiety over whether he would change his mind and offer an apology caused my knees to begin shaking again. Then something happened that changed my perception.

Pammy leaned in toward me and whispered into my ear, "Enjoy this day. You've been waiting a long time for this and it's finally here." Her comment brought me back to the meaning of the trial. Beyond receiving justice, it was about my peace of mind and holding him accountable. At that moment, I had to believe I would be OK whether I received an apology or not. The pain and darkness of the crime was finally exposed to the light, apology or no apology.

"This case is closed," announced the judge as he hit his gavel on the desk. There would be no apology for me.

The trial was over. The judge released the defense side of the gallery first, then he released our side to avoid any quarrels. There were many of us in the gallery, so it took some time for everyone to exit as I received hugs of support. Once we left the courtroom, the congratulatory gathering continued in the courthouse hallway.

Dad thanked our prosecuting attorneys immediately after stepping out of the courtroom. I saw people hugging, smiling, and crying, but I didn't feel the euphoria that everyone else felt. My closest friends just lost their father—there never was a win/win scenario for both families. "How do you feel Jenna?" asked Debra Bender. Searching for words, I glanced over and saw the joy on Mom and Dad's face. It made me smile. ". . . Pretty good," I said, giving her a hug and a "thank you."

Gratefulness filled my heart as I thought about all the other kids I met at the Children's Advocacy Center who didn't get the opportunity to go to trial, sit on the witness stand, or give a victim impact statement. I knew that not every survivor received the justice they deserved, and the survivors that did get to go to trial all had different experiences and outcomes.

Outside the doors of the courtroom a radio interviewer stood with a voice recorder. She asked if I could answer a few questions for her. She promised it would be a quick interview, and it was. In a daze I mumbled my way through it, not paying any attention to the station, angle of the interview, or when the interview aired. All I cared about was getting home, resting, and spending time with my family.

Lying in bed that night, not willing myself to sleep, my thoughts went every which way. *Was there something greater at work the past three days? Was it God's justice or people justice?* These questions and many more passed through my mind as I processed the last three days. I finally gave up and turned it all over to God, praying the most honest, down-to-earth prayer I had ever prayed.

CHAPTER 23

When Mr. Russell was sentenced to prison on November 10, 2004, our home phone seemed to ring continuously with calls from friends, casual acquaintances, and people we hadn't heard from in years—calls of encouragement, well wishing, or just kind words from caring people. Most of the time I let Dad handle the calls, and he seemed delighted to have those conversations.

The day after the sentencing I was talking with Mom in her bedroom when Dad joined us, showing a more pleasant demeanor than I had seen in months. I was holding one side of the sheet, helping Mom make the bed.

"Guess what?" he said.

"What?" Mom answered, without looking up.

"Listen to this," Dad said.

There was something about his voice, and his smile. I could feel a trickle of thrill pass through me. His enthusiasm was contagious.

He held his phone at arms length toward me and held his finger on the speaker button. "OK," he repeated. "Listen to this carefully."

"Please, Honey, just play the message," Mom begged.

I sat down on the bed and got comfortable. Dad pushed the play button on the recording for us to hear a pleasant-sounding male voice introducing himself as Steve Blow, a columnist for the *Dallas Morning News*. The name, Steve Blow, was no stranger to our household. My parents read his column every weekend and often commented about it. During the short recording Mr. Blow explained that he wanted to write a personal story about the sexual abuse I had experienced. Dad pushed the stop button and waited for our responses.

There was a short pause while I tried to wrap my head around everything I had just heard. "Was that really him?" I was so filled with disbelief, and maybe tingled with excitement. *Why would a renowned columnist want to do a story in the* Dallas Morning News *about me?*

"Yep, that's him. And he sounds anxious to meet you and get your story out to the public!" Dad said.

I moved off my comfortable perch on the bed and stood closer to where both Mom and Dad stood. Mom broke the silence when she suddenly added, "Oh, this could be huge, Jenna." I didn't have a clue what she was talking about, so I just let it stand.

"I'm sure Steve has read most of the court records, but he wants you to tell your story in person," Dad said. "Don't worry," he went on. "You don't have to say anything that makes you uncomfortable. I've read Steve's column every week since we've lived in the Dallas area. He's a true professional."

Hugging both of them and promising to let them know, "Really soon—probably tomorrow," I left the room to be alone.

I was still feeling a total brain drain from the events of the trial. Already, it seemed, I had told half the world about what I went through. Just thinking about reliving it all over again with the other half of the world made me feel weak all over. *Was I even capable of doing it, and did I even want to share it with the general public?*

The *Dallas Morning News* was the most widely distributed newspaper in the Dallas/Fort Worth Metroplex. Thousands of people would read about the events of my trauma. I had a serious choice to make. My story was not something I ever wanted sensationalized in any way, shape, or form.

I am not a compulsive person by nature, nor do I have a desire to draw attention to myself, so I slept on the offer and prayed for guidance. The next day I walked downstairs to tell Dad my decision: "I want to do the interview, so other kids can get help from their abuse, too." Dad gave me a hug. With both his hands stretched out on my shoulders, he looked me straight in the eye and asked me again if I was sure about my choice. I raised my chin up and said, "I'm sure. Go ahead and call him so we can schedule a time for the interview."

Dad went straight to the phone. A few minutes later he confirmed that the interview was scheduled for tomorrow at our house.

I had been through a lot, finishing high school in just over three short years, coping with a traumatic court procedure, and feeling like I was starting upon a real recovery. And this very day, at age seventeen, I was filling out forms to be entered into my first year of college.

I should have been nervous—I wasn't. The day of my interview Mom and I opened the door together and invited the columnist into our house. We shook hands and then directed him toward the dining room table, where I wanted to do the interview.

At once, I had a quiet moment of feeling surreal, as I realized it was the same room I first spoke with the police when I reported the abuse. I never imagined I would be speaking with a newspaper columnist about it. We talked small talk for a few minutes alone until Mom stepped into the room and offered Mr. Blow cookies that she baked just for the occasion.

I didn't want my parents to be present during the interview—they had enough painful reminders the past few days. They moved to an adjoining room, to eavesdrop, I later learned.

Mr. Blow thanked me from the start and told me how impressed he was that I had agreed to do the interview, saying, "What I've learned in all of my years of being a columnist is that most victims aren't willing to talk about their experiences." That said, he leaned over and recovered a little black voice recorder from his briefcase. It really stood out against the white tablecloth. "Please tell me if you're not comfortable with answering any of these questions," he stated. After he covered the encouragement and the disclaimer, he asked me the first question.

Even though I went into the interview with confidence, it was hard not to be a little anxious. However, he had such a warm personality that it was no time at all before I relaxed, reasoning with myself that a story in the newspaper was not that big a deal.

"So, Jenna, tell me about your life growing up and about school?" I told him about my family and about attending a private Christian school. Then he asked me about the Russells and how close we were with them. I explained how Mr. Russell was like family to me and how he groomed me with a slow step-by-step process with one goal in mind.

"How did you cope with everything?" he asked.

I explained that I tried my best to handle it on my own, while my parents were living in their own world of panic, anxiety, and grief, trying to find help for me from professionals outside the family. I mentioned the emergency room visits from hives, and the many doctor appointments to test my thyroid, test for anemia, and test for allergies. I told him that the doctors diagnosed my condition as "stress." "It was all about minimizing and denial. I didn't connect my coping behaviors with the abuse."

"Jenna, why didn't you feel you could tell anyone what was happening to you?"

I had a feeling this question was coming. "I didn't feel I could tell for lots of reasons," I said. I elaborated on how I felt it would somehow be my fault if I told and messed up the relationship with the Russells. I continued to do most of the talking from that point, telling him about my sister, Stephanie, demanding the truth, and went on from there, right up to the end of the trial.

"How do you feel now," he said, "I mean about Mark Russell being sentenced to prison?"

"I slept so-o-o-o well last night, but the sentencing didn't change the damage that was done. Just because I received justice doesn't mean I healed overnight. There are still hurts left to be healed. It did allow me to see more plainly that his actions were a serious crime since I had minimized it so much in my head for so long." I went on to explain how grateful I was to receive justice, and how most children, unfortunately, don't get the satisfaction of seeing justice served.

"What would you tell other victims out there that have experienced abuse?"

Thinking for a moment, I chose my words carefully. "Tell. Find a way to tell someone. Whether the abuse is current or in the past, put aside your feelings of shame and fear, find someone you trust and tell. . . . Don't wait 'just for the right time.' Speak up."

After the interview, we said our good-byes. Seemingly

pleased with the interview, Mr. Blow looked at me and said, "Thank you for sharing your story. And don't worry, I won't put your name in the article. It's our policy not to name sexual assault victims and most victims don't want their names mentioned anyway."

Then Dad chimed in and said, "Yeah, please, don't put her name in the article."

Almost immediately after they both agreed to leave my name out of the story, I shouted, "No!"

My full-blown reaction, as if it had sprung from my mouth from somewhere else, dumbfounded me. They just looked at me, with equally blank expressions, waiting for something. . . .

"The purpose of me agreeing to do this story is to help other victims. You asked me to address victims at the end of the article. I encouraged them to be brave, speak up, and get help for themselves. How can I ask them to do that if I'm too ashamed to list *my* name as a victim? I can't ask them to do something and not demonstrate it."

For what seemed like a long time, they just stared at me, speechless. Finally, Dad said, "Well that's a good point, but it's whatever you feel comfortable with."

Mr. Blow was not quick to agree. "Just to be sure, I'm going to give you more time to think about it. I'll contact you before we publish and you can let me know," he said.

He turned to put away the recorder, which gave me a pause to think before saying, "Maybe you could put my number in there, too, so that if someone is struggling they can call me and I can help encourage them."

I started to say something else when Dad interrupted me. "OK, Jenna, I think that's too much, if you do that there's no telling *who* might call you."

Mr. Blow gave a sigh of relief. "Thanks, Greg," he said, "you're so right about the phone calls."

After I thanked Mr. Blow again for his willingness to write the story, we all walked him out the door and waved goodbye.

Talking with Mom and Dad after the interview, it was easy to learn they had eavesdropped. "It went well. He asked good questions," I said. We discussed how the final published article might read. We wouldn't have to wait long. He planned to publish the article within the next couple days. I felt a sense of energy like never before after the interview. Boldness emerged and a flame of passion was lit in my heart that day.

My prayer was that the article would reach the abused and encourage them to get help. After he asked again, I gave Mr. Blow the OK to use my name in the newspaper article. On November 14, 2004, the article was published in the Sunday edition, the most popular paper-reading day of the week. True to his word, he published my name. The title of the article read, "*To get peace, she knew she needed to tell.*"

After the article was published, our home phone rang from an unknown number. Cautiously putting the phone to my ear, I heard heavy crying and gasping sounds as if someone was trying to talk through a projected crying spell. Soon a woman's voice cried, "I'm so sorry, Jenna. I used to work with Mark Russell, and I just had to call after reading about what happened to you. I can't tell you my name because I still work at the same place where I knew Mark, but I feel horrible after learning about what he put you through. If I had only exposed him from the start, you could've been spared."

She paused enough for me to say, "That's OK, just tell me what happened."

"I can't tell you everything, but it went on for a while. It wasn't as bad as what you went through but I needed that job, and I was a nervous wreck, not knowing what would happen next or if my supervisor would find out and blame me. I had no idea he was hurting anyone else, but I should've known. I knew him well, and I didn't like anything about him." She cleared her throat. "Oh, Jenna, I'm so sorry."

Even though she didn't go through the same physical torture inflicted upon me, I could still empathize with her, believing she must be suffering with some of my own feelings of guilt and embarrassment.

After hanging up the phone, I was visibly shaking with outrage. *Maybe there were more than just two victims?* Mr. Russell lived in other states and coached other basketball teams throughout his life. *How many more of his victims were out there suffering in a world of silence?*

Feedback from the article didn't stop with the lady on the phone. Various people wrote the columnist and thanked him for writing the story and raising awareness about child sexual abuse. My willingness to speak out as a teenage victim rendered positive feedback. Overall I felt good about the article, especially since Mr. Blow honored my request and included my name. Mom bought more copies than I could count and sent them to family. They weren't embarrassed that it happened, so I wasn't. I was grateful to have their support after revealing the abuse. It encouraged me to hear that people were desperate to learn more about this devastating issue.

Sitting, L to R: Jenna at age 18, holding Gypsy, Jenna's mother, Kellie, and sister Lauren. Standing, L to R: Daniel, Stephanie's fiancé, Stephanie, and Jenna's father, Greg, posing for *Glamour Magazine*, October 2005.

Dan Leal, executive director of the Children's Advocacy Center of Denton County, where I received counseling, called a few weeks after reading my story in the paper to ask if I would consider being the honorary speaker at the CACDC National Crime Victims' Rights Week event, April 21, 2005. Feeling incredibly honored, I eagerly accepted the invitation. However, he asked me to think about it and let him know if I felt comfortable with the appearance.

I called Mr. Leal a week later and said, "People need to hear there is hope and healing after abuse. If my story can inspire just one person and make people believe there is hope, then I'm all in."

Over two hundred people, including the Denton County District Attorney, attended my morning presentation at the very courthouse where I sat on the witness stand. This time I didn't speak on the witness stand as a victim, I spoke from the podium as a victor. After my presentation, the audience gave a standing ovation. I was overwhelmed—I never saw myself as bold or brave, as others did.

CHAPTER 24

Toward the end of March 2006, a celebratory attitude about finishing my first year at Collin County Community College began to materialize. Giving it my all proved to be what I hoped for and I secretly envisioned this as my "getting back to normal" year. Through facing the emotional effects of abuse in counseling and a renewed faith in Christ, I successfully stopped taking all my medications. This was the year my change of attitude and emotional strength seemed to just sneak up on me. Mom and Dad were on an upswing, too.

My study schedule was set in stone for the coming six weeks of school until a phone call interrupted my study period and started a series of events that would change the course of my life in a way I couldn't have dreamed. The call was from Mr. Leal with another invitation for me to be one of two speakers at the CACDC's Tenth Annual Community Breakfast.

He said the other speaker for the event was Texas State Senator Jane Nelson, an active advocate for children's safety and health. The speaking engagement was scheduled for April 6, my birthday. After thanking him for the invitation, I promised to confirm my decision in a day or two. *Wow! What a memora-*

ble day that would be, I thought—*speaking at The University of North Texas for the Children's Advocacy Center on my nineteenth birthday.*

Now, with almost two successful semesters of college behind me, a new outlook on life, and an invitation to speak before hundreds of people for children's advocacy, I felt like a new person—maybe the real me, with a new sense of joy and hope. And, most of all, I had developed a new, prayerful relationship with God.

All these feelings of intense happiness and excitement passed through me in the first adrenaline rush. Then, in about the same amount of time, most of these feelings of well-being were diminished with self-doubt. *Am I getting way ahead of myself with school finals in a few weeks? Can I really control my shaky knees enough to speak before hundreds of people expecting to be informed and inspired by a nineteen-year-old college student?* My heart was racing, picturing myself performing in a situation I couldn't have possibly dreamed. The answer was no, not without some divine guidance.

I was alone in my bedroom, studying, when I took the call from Mr. Leal. After the excitement died down, I sat on my bed for a few minutes, wondering if I could really do this, before dropping to my knees and laying everything out in a prayer to God, asking for guidance and confidence to speak before so many people about the personal and traumatic details of my past. When my prayer was finished, I had my answer.

My heart was in my throat, but my steps were lighter as I casually walked downstairs and told my parents my decision to speak at the breakfast. "Oh, Jenna, I'm so proud of you. You're going to do great." Mom's hands covered her face.

Dad put on a broad smile. They both hugged me and there

was a moment of silence before I asked them if they would come to hear me speak.

"Yes, we'll be there." Mom spoke for both of them.

I had classes most of the next day, so I asked Dad to call Mr. Leal and inform him of my decision to speak at the breakfast.

After arriving home from classes that same day, Dad told me, "Dan was thrilled to hear that you've accepted the invitation to speak at the breakfast. And there's more. He's doing a radio interview after the breakfast to raise public awareness about sexual abuse and he's invited you to speak on the air with him. Dan reminded me that April is Child Abuse Prevention Month, and he wants to get the word out to as many people as possible."

"I'm really excited to do the show," I said, "but I can't help but be nervous. Then, there's the radio talk show right afterward. . . . I'll talk to my professors and get excused from class for a day, and call Mr. Leal as early as possible tomorrow morning for the details."

My relationship with God was growing slowly as I trusted a little more each day that He could restore my broken pieces. I believed it, and I could feel it in my heart and soul as I put all I could into a long prayer before bedtime.

God, am I unconsciously lying to myself, thinking I can help others and raise awareness by exposing my own experience to the whole world? I can't heal people, but You can. Please use my experience to help others.

It was nearly impossible for me to focus on school with the annual community breakfast and radio interview in the back of my mind. Each night I tried to make my tone seem natural and unhurried—arranging and rearranging my notes, at the same time struggling with the reality of speaking in front of three hundred people and answering questions at a radio interview. I was nervous about the speech, but nothing compared to the jitters I felt about the radio interview—answering impromptu questions from a total stranger. Nevertheless, I gave my verbal commitment to Mr. Leal and I was not going to back down.

I woke up tired on April 6, feeling like I hardly slept at all—it would be a long day. While stumbling down the stairs, hoping for a miracle out of a cup of coffee, a million different thoughts raced through my head before I reached for an empty coffee cup. *How would the audience view me? They're adults, many of them professionals. How could they possibly take seriously anything a nineteen-year-old had to say on the subject?*

By the time my parents joined me for coffee, my anxious thoughts dissipated and I decided to just be myself and enjoy the whole thing. Anyway, everything was in order, from my speech right down to the shoes I would wear—I was doing the right thing.

Mom, Dad, and I made the forty-five minute drive to the University of North Texas Gateway Center, in Denton, Texas, for the 6:00 a.m. breakfast where I was scheduled to speak.

During the drive, Mom did her best to engage me in conversation, and encouraging words. I was still struggling with sore, sleepy eyes while going over my notes for the speech when Mom broke into my thoughts to ask me how I felt. I gulped and said, "Tired and nervous is not a good combination, but I'm as ready as I can be."

"Honey, they'll just be happy to see that someone made it through the court process successfully and is doing well," she said. Her words helped me to see the big picture. She went on to say, "Sexual abuse is not easy for anyone to talk about—almost a taboo subject and not a subject you hear in casual conversation. They'll probably be delighted to hear anything encouraging from you."

The size of the University Center scared me to the point that I could barely see or breathe. In my mind, I pictured a small classroom of people. I felt the nerves in my stomach tighten more. The feeling of nausea came over me as we continued to cross the parking lot and approach one of the many entrances to the center. Dad's comment of "Wow! This is really big," didn't help.

I saw Mr. Leal first thing as we entered the building. We talked briefly while he thanked me, handed me a printed program, and made sure I understood how the event would proceed. We were seated at the front next to Senator Jane Nelson.

My hands started to perspire a few minutes before Mr. Leal started the introductions. I hurried over to where the water and coffee were arranged on a table at the back of the room, grabbed a tall glass of water, and hurried back to my seat. Despite my best efforts to keep myself calm, my heart kept racing. I took in deep breaths as discretely as possible, trying not to look nervous.

After introducing the event speakers, Mr. Leal welcomed me again as the keynote speaker and, along with my parents, a recipient of services at the CACDC. He also mentioned that my perpetrator received a prison sentence. Finally, he said my name and welcomed me to the front of the room.

I looked at him with a closed-mouth smile and started what felt like a long walk to the center of the podium. The room was silent. I placed my feet in a firm position behind the podium and grabbed each side of the top of the podium with my left and right hand. After positioning myself, the first words out of my mouth were, "Hello . . . " then I paused. There was dead silence from the audience while I momentarily freaked out expecting them to return my greeting. Finally, I said, "My name is Jenna Quinn, and I'm very grateful to be here today to share my story with you."

My goal was to spread awareness about sexual abuse that would cause people to be more mindful of the serious nature of the crimes against children in their own communities, the state, and throughout the country. My message was short. In summary, I talked about Mark Russell and how he was a strategic perpetrator. I didn't feel comfortable going into details and didn't think it necessary. Then the focus of my topic shifted to how I sought services at the CACDC and how their services were beneficial. I also thanked the multidisciplinary teams and prosecutors that worked so hard on my case. My speech ended on an inspirational note and I explained how those who work to help bring justice and healing to children are planting seeds of hope. I talked about my physical and emotional healing and life's current fulfillment.

I tried not to be distracted by the faces people were making in the audience. Some people were scowling and others were smiling. Mainly people were blinking and staring back at me. I said, "Thank you," then walked back to my seat amidst a standing ovation and a long round of applause. Even with the immediate adrenaline rush and a momentary sense of a new identity, I returned to my seat on wobbly knees. The acceptance and encouragement I received soothed my serious frame of mind, and helped me to believe my message was well received.

The radio station, where I would speak next, was a long drive from the University Gateway Center. During the trip, my parents and I discussed my presentation at the community breakfast. "Of course," Mom cheered, "your dad and I loved it, and your audience seemed to hang on every word. But the big question is, how do *you* feel?"

"I think it went well. I didn't mess up much, except for one long pause, where I lost my place in my notes, and I started looking for a place to hide."

"Speakers use long pauses for emphasis, and it works," Mom said. "Your pause didn't seem out of place at all."

"Anyway," Dad said, "even experienced speakers don't expect to give perfect performances every time. You did great, and you'll get better." Dad put on a mischievous smile and continued, "I can still remember when you first learned to ride a bike. That wasn't a perfect performance, either, Honey."

When we arrived at the radio station, the receptionist signed us in, and we followed her down a hallway to the recording room. I glanced at the walls in the hallway and saw pictures of framed hit records, one after the other, signed by their artists.

Experiencing both excitement and nerves, I had an urgent need to write out all my answers as the interviewer went over the questions before recording, but there was no time. The interviewer stated Mr. Leal would speak first. It was easy to see how relaxed Mr. Leal was with everything, which allowed me a small ray of confidence.

Before putting on our headphones, the interviewer looked at me, with a knowing smile, and said, "Just do your best to relax. You will be surprised how well you do."

My hands were wet when the button was pushed to start the recorder.

Raising awareness about child sexual abuse was the purpose of the radio interview, and my contribution was from the perspective of a survivor, especially expressing the difficulty in making an outcry. Dan would give a professional perspective on how the CACDC catered to survivors' needs, including mine. I was allowed three minutes for my responses. I can't remember how long Mr. Leal talked, but it seemed much longer than three minutes.

Dan answered questions about societal statistics and how often children self-disclose about ¡sexual abuse.

The first question to me was, "Why do abused children find it so difficult to tell?" I heard my voice as clear and confident—despite my zoning-out time—I was now in my element, explaining that the perpetrator who sexually abuses a child is most likely abusing that particular child because they *know* the child and the child's family. I mentioned how in many cases, including my own, the families of the child are also groomed to trust the perpetrator.

"It's extremely difficult for a child to tell on someone they know everyone trusts, because they feel the blame will be put back on them. But that's just one reason for their fear of telling, and, in my own case, that was just one of *many* reasons. Even if a child makes it through the initial outcry, the lives of whole families are sometimes put into jeopardy, lifelong friendships can be destroyed with blame, heartache, financial hardship, and the list goes on and on."

I explained how abused children feel alone in their pain, but reiterated that they are *not* alone in their pain. I pleaded that if a child, or even an older person hasn't told yet, it didn't matter what their age, they needed to tell and get help. "Don't waste another day living in pain." I concluded by talking about how telling was the first step to my healing.

On the ride home, I reflected on the interview, realizing that it was not about me, "Jenna the survivor." It was about *empowering others to become survivors* of sexual abuse. And it made me ask myself what it meant to be a survivor. A survivor is often referred to as someone who remains alive (heart still beating) after an event in which others have died. Often, I heard sexual abuse referred to as a "death of the spirit." From my experience I define a survivor of sexual abuse as someone who has confronted the abuse and works to emotionally bring their spirit back to a place of life again (freedom). The reason one survives is because they do not let their spirit stay broken or in a state of death but rather consciously pursue healing.

I was in love with addressing the socially taboo subject. Before our trip was over, my purpose became clearer—raise awareness about child sexual abuse to prevent it and inspire those being abused to get help. I knew then that I could not be silent.

CHAPTER 25

After my first year of junior college there was never any serious doubt in my mind what I wanted to study. My passion was to understand more about human nature and my goal was to work with abused children in some capacity. In spring 2007 I was able to transfer to the University of Texas at Dallas (UTD).

It felt wonderful—I was finally standing on solid ground looking the whole world in the face, it seemed, with a fresh and new perspective on everything. The two years at a junior college gave me ample time to ponder about what course would lead me along the path of fulfilling my new goal in life. At UTD I majored in psychology, and I was already thinking about what choices were available for interning during my senior year.

I didn't know it at the time, but this choice would take my life in an unexpected direction and purpose.

My junior year involved a full load of college courses while cramming in summer classes when possible. Reading, studying, and losing myself in writing papers was something I enjoyed. The library felt like my second home. When I wasn't doing school-work, I spent time making new friends or being with my family at home and on vacations. By the beginning of my senior year of college, I was feeling mentally burnt out but optimistic about my upcoming internship.

My internship would start the spring semester of 2008, and because I took the equivalent of one full semester of summer courses, I would graduate UTD in December.

On the first day of class, my professor gave out a list of places where we could fulfill our internship hours. He advised us to choose an organization that matched our career program interest. From almost the beginning of my studies at UTD, my heart was set on interning at the CACDC. My heart dropped to the floor when I didn't see it listed as an option.

I asked my professor if he could grant an exception, allowing me to intern at the CACDC. My professor said granting the exception would have to be coordinated first with CACDC officials, which would take some time. I then asked for and was given permission to talk with CACDC's executive director, Dan Leal, about my wishes.

That afternoon, I contacted Mr. Leal by phone and asked if I could intern at the center for school credit. He explained that they were not on the university's list for a reason—CACDC internships consisted of graduate students only. He wasn't sure if there was any real work for me there. He also questioned my enthusiasm about interning and if I was emotionally ready.

"I'll look into this, but are you sure you want to come here every week for an entire semester? The cases might be difficult for you, and I just want to make sure that you're emotionally prepared," he said. I didn't hesitate.

"I'm sure," I replied.

He made me promise to tell if at any point the internship was too overwhelming. I assured him I would tell him or a counselor if anything brought back "triggers" or caused post-traumatic stress.

"Alright, I'll ask the counselors and see if we can find work for you here," he said.

A week later, I received the much anticipated phone call from Mr. Leal. "Well, Jenna, how'd you like to be the very first undergraduate intern to complete hours at the Children's Advocacy Center of Denton County?"

I giggled with relief. "I would love to."

He said I had to do two things before starting the internship. First, I needed to talk to their lead counselor about my expectations, and second, determine the areas where I wanted to gain the most field experience. After talking with the counselor, she would help put my schedule together.

I spoke with my professor, giving him the information he wanted and informing him that the CACDC's executive director granted me permission to fulfill hours there. My professor said he would contact Dan to confirm and then have a final answer for me by the next class period.

Mom and Dad had mixed feelings about whether or not it was a good idea to intern at the center. I understood their point of view, however, I couldn't explain my intense desire to be there—most of which I couldn't put into words. I only knew about child sexual abuse from my own experiences and wanted to help save kids somehow from the torment I endured.

The following day I was the first to arrive in class, hoping for an answer. Running my questions together, I asked my professor, "Were you able to reach Mr. Leal? Has the Psychology Department approved me to intern there?"

"The Department did clear the Children's Advocacy Center as a place for you to fulfill your internship hours." He was smiling.

Trying to contain my excitement and joy, I said, "Thank you. I'm really looking forward to it." When sitting at my desk, it felt like I was sitting on a cushion of air, about two feet above my seat. I may as well have skipped the rest of my classes that day, because working at the CACDC was all I could think about.

Right after class, I called Mr. Leal and told him I was approved. We discussed my first start day and my availability. My classes at UTD were scheduled from eight in the morning until two in the afternoon. From three to six o clock, three days a week, I would work at the CACDC. When I told Mom and Dad, they congratulated me and offered their moral support. However, they also asked me to make the same promise: to tell them if I struggled there emotionally. I gave them my word, assuring them everything would be OK regardless of the outcome.

"I have to do this," I said.

My stomach felt tight sitting quietly in my car in the CACDC parking lot on my first day of interning, feeling the anxieties and anxiousness of what was to come. I reminded myself that it was probably just typical "first day on the job jitters." Finally, I grabbed my binder and headed toward the door. After passing security in the building, the head counselor, Rose Boehm, met me in the hallway.

She smiled at me and said, "Welcome. We're so happy to have you as an intern." She was the one I received court preparation services from for the trial. She introduced me to all of the graduate interns and gave a tour of the center.

L to R: Counselor Rose Boehm, Jenna, and CACDC Director Dan Leal at the Children's Advocacy Center during Jenna's internship. The teddy bears are given to patients as a physical reminder of the support offered by the CACDC.

Next came the introductions to the multidisciplinary team, the police officers on staff, investigators, SANE nurse, family coordinators, counselors, and forensic interviewers. I was in awe of how each multidisciplinary professional communicated on behalf of each child's case. I learned that each child was treated on a case-by-case basis since every child's case was different. Reality started to set in as to how much work goes into each child receiving healing and justice.

At the end of our tour, Counselor Boehm said, "Our staff all know that you came here for services, but you won't be treated as such. You'll be recognized as Jenna, the intern, not Jenna, the client."

"That's exactly what I wanted, thank you."

The rest of my hours for the day were spent in the intern room, getting acquainted with each intern as they briefly told me about themselves and what they used the room for. They each explained their preferred clinical method of therapy and why they chose to use certain therapy techniques. I took notes in my binder to share with my class at UTD, a required assignment— write journal entries of my experiences.

As the weeks went by, I came to understand why Mr. Leal was concerned about my emotional state so soon after starting my recovery. Gut-wrenching child abuse cases taught me first-hand how rampant sexual and other abuse seemingly goes unnoticed. At different times during my stay at the center, Mr. Leal and Rose gave me permission to walk away from it if I became too emotionally upset. However, I never once gave the option of quitting any serious consideration. Working with abused children was my calling.

During one of my days at the center, a young girl caught my attention. She was about my age at the time my abuse started. As I walked down the hall, I overheard some of the counselors talking about her situation and coping mechanisms. She was dealing with her sexual abuse in some of the same ways I coped. Again, I found myself talking with Rose. She helped me separate myself from the familiarity of the little girl's story. Rose advised me to take a week off. "Just for a break," she said. Without any hesitation, that's exactly what I did. It would give me time to separate from the cases and decompress my various emotions.

During that week, I prayed fervently about my feelings, wanting to be strong enough to handle the internship, but I felt so weak. *Couldn't my passion get me through?* I prayed for God to give me strength and reminded myself that I didn't have to do things on my own strength anymore. God was there to help me. I recalled a passage of scripture that read: *My grace is sufficient for you, for my power is made perfect in weakness.* This was my verse of reference on several occasions.

Doubled-up in my efforts to continue my internship, I made the choice to make up the hours missed from taking a week off. I continued to ask the counselors as many questions as I could, without being a nuisance. The more facts and information learned, the better I felt, and it allayed some of my anxieties—at least temporarily.

Statistics involving children sexually abused before the age of eighteen sickened me. I became consumed in thought on how to create a solution to prevent it—the "silver bullet" to end it all. Something had to be changed. And, something *could be changed,* I thought. The more I encountered horrific cases of little innocent children each week at the center, the more I became convinced there was a better way of preventing much of what I saw there. *But, how?* That was the question that stayed with me.

The children that walked into the center came because the abuse had already occurred in their lives. With every new kid that stepped through the doors, I had an overall feeling of defeat. We were all too late. The damage was already done. I thought to myself, *Why aren't we preventing this from happening in the first place?* The center was left with the aftermath of trying to heal them and, thank goodness, was doing a good job. This place will always have a special meaning for me. Not just because I received services, but it was there, among the painful stories, that I envisioned a better way to help protect children from the trauma of child sexual abuse.

My next day at the center seemed to be just an ordinary day of waking up as a tired college student, attending classes, and then going to my internship, until a particular child's case struck a serious nerve with me. I noticed a young girl standing in the hallway who looked about four years old. She stayed on my mind. So, I waited for the right moment to ask one of the counselors about her. Meanwhile, my anxiousness to know more about this girl somewhat faded as I walked the halls and checked to see if other departments needed my help. During my walk, my question was answered. I saw this little girl again. This time, she was in the play therapy room.

She had two therapy dolls, one male and one female. The counselor sat across from her on the floor. Using the dolls, the little girl showed the counselor specifically how she was sexually assaulted. I watched as she directed the dolls' movements quickly, taking off all the clothes of the dolls and acting out the assaults. Her gestures burned in my mind. My face grew warm with anger. I wasn't sure how much more of all this I could take.

This little girl wasn't old enough to know that the sexual abuse committed against her was a criminal act. I found out later that for her it was an everyday normal occurrence. This was the last straw for me. I said a silent prayer in my head to calm myself down and ended it with uttering, "Lord, what can I do to help? Please use me."

When I rushed back into the intern room, I asked the first intern by the door, "How can you do this as a career?"

Wide-eyed from my abruptness she said, "It's a rewarding line of work. We get to be a part of their healing process, and maybe the only people who support them." Then she said, "I've been here two years and seen a lot of these cases and yes, it's difficult sometimes, but worth it. What I don't understand is how you hold up after seeing some of these kids, knowing what you've been through."

I paused to think and took a seat. "If I hadn't forgiven my offender I wouldn't be able to do this. This hasn't been a walk in the park for me. But I just know this is where I need to be right now."

That evening I told Mom the story about the doll and the little girl. "I feel so discouraged. I want to do more than intern to help these kids."

"If you want to do more," Mom said, "there's a lot you can do. Anything is possible with God on your side."

That night, I prayed about it, tossed and turned, and prayed about it some more. I prayed, over and over, in so many different ways to get a "clearer picture of what to do if I'm supposed to help."

CHAPTER 26

When I awoke the next morning it felt like another ordinary day—put my feet on the floor, rub sleep out of my eyes, shower, and everything else that goes with "ordinary" for a college student. Even now, as I write this, a smile is ready to break over my lips at referring to this particular day as "ordinary" because this day was one of the most memorable times in my personal battle to get the word out about child sexual abuse.

While eating a quick breakfast before leaving for my first class, I was still thinking about Mom's encouraging words from the night before, "If you want to do more, there's a lot you can do." And I was still thinking about her statement that afternoon at the clinic when a helpless feeling overcame me. I felt so small remembering that I went there as a client. There was so much work to be done. I stood just inside the entrance and said a quiet prayer, for me, not for the kids; "Lord, I don't ask why bad things happen, or to understand everything, but only that You direct my steps so I can help."

It was early so I strolled through the corridor and down a hallway to a particular wall that I passed every day. This wall was lined with multiple shelves of teddy bears for children to take home after their first visit. I was given one of these little bears, too, and I still treasure her—Angel. Remembering my own experience with Angel, I imagined children cuddled with their bear at night when they felt alone or afraid. This was the purpose of the bears: security and comfort for children.

My mind wandered in thought as I continued to stare at the bears on the shelves: *eight hours or less in bed cuddled with a little teddy bear, seven to eight hours in school, and God only knows what horrors they faced during the interim before crying out for help.*

The perpetrator embedded within family relationships still awaited some of them when they left the center. It sickened me to face the truth: we saw these children a couple of times a week, then slipped into our cars and drove home to a safe environment while the children left the clinic and often returned to a house filled with hurtful memories.

As I stared at the wall, this time with a different perspective, my mind was finally made up. There had to be a better way to protect these kids, and I knew right then the subject wouldn't leave my mind until there was a resolution. It was a long shot at best, but I had a revelation: what if students, teachers, parents, and other influential people in the community were informed about this seemingly taboo thing called "child sexual abuse"? If the right people realized what percentage of children are affected by child sexual abuse before the age of eighteen, would they support an effort to require schools to teach prevention? It's a crime that kids and teachers should have knowledge of in order to report.

The rest of the day my head was spinning. In my young mind it seemed so logical and plain common sense—just pass something to make it an educational requirement along with all the other requirements for schools. Simple. *Well, maybe not so sim-*

ple, I thought. *If it were that easy, someone in the legislature would have already done it.*

I was too excited about this crazy idea to make much sense out of it. So, during the drive home from the center, I tried to calm myself before entering the house, because I just *had* to talk to Mom and Dad. Mom was a fourth-grade teacher and Dad was a college graduate and a smart businessman. Maybe they could convince me that I'm not crazy. We all shared equally my pain and heartache throughout my ordeal, and I trusted their judgment more than anyone in the world. *Who else to help me start the ball rolling—if it would roll at all?*

As we sat at the dinner table that night, my enthusiasm, frustrating thoughts, and concerns about the matter ran rampant. I blurted out, "I've had some tough days at the center, but they all got worked out." I also mentioned that Mom was right to feel my internship was for a good purpose—that got their attention. "Go on," Mom said in such a way that it encouraged me to open up more. I told them about some of the cases I saw and how emotional they made me feel. Then I explained my idea for legislation that would require schools to be a place to reach children in a way that would *prevent* child sexual abuse. Mom's eyes lit up. "Oh, my gosh! That is doable! We just had someone come into the classroom today to talk to the kids on how a bill becomes a law."

"Really?" I asked.

Mom started, "Jenna, that is such a great idea. We have so many outside speakers come to our school to teach prevention classes like fire prevention, accident prevention, and so many others . . . , but this would be the first to teach children how to prevent sexual abuse and tell if it's happened. It's the most disgusting epidemic in our society and not a word is spoken about it in our classrooms." She went on to say, "When I read that pamphlet in the waiting room I couldn't believe it. I wish someone had given me that pamphlet sooner. I'm an educator and a parent and was completely ignorant of your symptoms. Parents and teachers need to understand what to look out for."

Adding to what she said, I brought up the simple fact that none of my schools ever warned us about the way perpetrators groom their victims or discussed the dangers of sexual abuse or offered us the opportunity to tell. "But, if it could be discussed in school, in an informal setting, maybe kids would feel comfortable telling about their experiences. They at least need a *chance* to tell."

Before our family discussion was over, we were all high on the idea. Mom suggested approaching Mr. Leal with the subject. Dad nodded in agreement, saying, "I'm sure Dan knows some of the right people to contact."

That night, I was upbeat from hearing such encouragement from both my parents. Yet, having the courage to vocalize these ideas to others was something else. I wondered if Mr. Leal and the other staff at the center would think I was delusional. That night in bed I conjured up several different scenarios in my head of how I would present the idea.

The drive from UTD to the center was a minimum of thirty minutes, depending on traffic. This day, the ride seemed exceptionally long. Arriving at the center, I sat inside the car for a few moments, feeling sleep deprived and fighting off fatigue. Talking to myself I said, "It's going to be a great day. I'm here for a reason." I walked into the center with a smile on my face and hoped for the best.

Several things were happening in the internship room when I reported for my assigned duties that day. Counselors quickly moved in and out of the room engaging in various conversations and consultations. One of the counselors put her hand on my shoulder and said, "Jenna, we're really going to need your help today. Some of the interns couldn't make it in."

Although it was a busy day, I made up my mind that I wanted to tell Mr. Leal about my idea before the end of my shift. But, I didn't know his schedule for the day. He was a busy man and sometimes I didn't see him at all. I asked several counselors if they knew when he was available. No help there. Then I decided to ask Rose. I walked down a short hall to her office, knocked lightly on the door, and tiptoed in.

I asked her if she would check Mr. Leal's schedule for a time when I could speak with him. "Let me check . . . " her words came slowly. "Yep, you're in." She finally said, "You got it. In about an hour he has a break."

Waiting in the intern room to speak with Mr. Leal felt like waiting to open gifts on Christmas morning. Finally, I looked at my watch for the last time, announced I'd be "right back," and hurried out the door.

As I walked to his office, I breathed in deeply. My palms were sweaty from a combination of nerves and too much caffeine. His office door was cracked open. I knocked gently on the door a few times until I heard him say, "Come on in." He greeted me with a warm smile as I stepped into this office. "How's everything going?"

"It's going good," I said, trying to make my words sound casual. He asked me to have a seat.

I eased into a big leather chair, sat up straight, crossed my knees, and placed my hands in my lap. He started off by saying the other interns enjoyed having me at the clinic. I assured him that I loved getting to know each one and they handled answering all my questions well. *Just say it Jenna, he doesn't have a lot of time,* I thought to myself. Nervous now, I cleared my throat and said, "Being here has been really hard at times, but it's also been reassuring. I'm able to see how the center operates and how each child's case is dealt with." I looked down at the floor, then raised my head to look into his eyes and continued, "The cases are difficult to hear about. Some of them have reminded me too much of my own experience."

He continued to listen as I said, "I want to change the amount of children that come here because they come in *after* the abuse has occurred."

"We do some prevention work in the community with trainings, but for the most part we deal with healing and justice after the fact," he replied.

With a serious but optimistic tone, I cleared my throat and said, "I have some ideas on how we can change the prevention side of things."

I wasn't nervous anymore. I had said it. But I paused and inhaled a long breath and let it all out before continuing, "What if there was a law in place that required all school teachers to receive training so they can recognize child sexual abuse symptoms? And every school should be required to show students how to recognize when they are being groomed for sexual abuse." I had to stop here for a few seconds to gauge Mr. Leal's reaction to, what must have seemed as, my outburst of emotion.

His expression never changed, nor did he offer any comments. He finally said, "Go on, Jenna, you have my full attention."

"From my own experience," I said, "I've come to realize there must be hundreds or even thousands of children out there suffering in the silence of shame every day with no idea that it's OK to even tell close friends or their parents, *especially* their parents." Then I went on to explain how the student training was just as important as the teacher training.

Mr. Leal was silent for what felt like ten minutes. Then he nodded his head in agreement, leaned in closer, and said, "Well, how would you do that?"

I explained that I didn't exactly know and needed to research. "I just think that kids need the chance to tell someone in a place outside their home. And at school they have a teacher and a counselor."

Mr. Leal folded his hands in front of him, leaned forward with his elbows on top of his desk, and stared at me with a blank expression. "Your idea has merit, but are you sure you want to pursue this?" he finally asked.

"Yeah, I do. But are you on board to help if I can do the leg work?"

"If you're still committed to this idea in a couple of days, we can talk again. But, keep your thinking cap on. And as you think, just know, what you have in mind is a slow, tedious, frustrating process. You'll be dealing with the Texas State Education Agency, state House of Representatives, state senators, and you may be called upon to lobby. So, what I'm saying is, you may want to spend some time reading about the whole process before you get started."

I had only figured on keeping Mr. Leal fifteen or twenty minutes, max. Time was lost on me, but I said everything I wanted to say and it felt good. I stood, trying to hold back some of my exuberance, and said, "Thank you, Mr. Leal."

He stood and shook my hand. "What we've discussed could be a first. And if your heart is really into it, how could anyone stand against you?"

A flash of satisfaction, mixed with inspiration, shot through me as I left his office. That evening, I could hardly wait until we were at the dinner table to tell Mom and Dad about my conversation with Mr. Leal.

Mom was first to declare her approval. I knew she wanted to hug me because that's what she always did. This time she remained seated, squeezed my hands, and said, "Honey, I'm so excited for you."

Dad maintained his silent and pleasant look about his face while hearing my explanation. When dinner was over, he pushed his chair away from the table with a scraping sound of wood against tile. He looked straight at me for a second before standing, "Jenna, what you're proposing sounds great, but how in the world can you do this while you carry a full load of college credits, work at the center, and have any time for yourself?"

"I can handle school and the workload, Dad. Once I learn the ropes on how to approach it, I can ask for help from Mr. Leal and others, and see how it goes from there. This is really important to me. If it's doable, then someone needs to do it, and it may as well be me."

Dad suggested I do some research on how the Texas State legislature is structured, take down names, use the computer, and make some calls. "You're going to have to start somewhere."

"Great idea," I said and excused myself as I pushed away from the table.

For research, I was limited in my resources. I didn't have my own computer, so I used the family computer in the office room at home for everything, including school papers. After leaving the dinner table I scurried over to the computer room to look up representatives and senators in the nearby districts. I read their biographies, noting their committee involvement and areas of interest.

After a couple of hours of research, I lost my momentum. So far, I didn't know if I had found the right person, but I was too tired to let it consume me anymore. *At least I got the ball rolling,* I thought. I was not scheduled back at the center until the following week, so I had more time to study my options.

In the meantime, I thought about how the semester was approaching its end. There were only a few more weeks before finals so I had to start studying, and finish strong. As I lay in bed that evening, I thanked God for the support of others in my life. I was going to need it. I had no idea what I was getting myself into and how much it would cost me in time, energy, and personal sacrifice.

CHAPTER 27

Indecision, self-doubt, and worry were replaced with a new sense of confidence, joy, and hope after my visit with Mr. Leal and the roundtable discussion with Mom and Dad. I started thinking like a new person with a new faith in God. I was blessed with new friends, new goals, and a totally different perspective on life.

My turnaround wasn't spontaneous; when I started to pray truly believing in the power of God and His ability to grant my prayer requests, things started to happen. I felt guided to make my new life goal about doing everything I could to protect children from sexual abuse. I firmly believed God would lead me in a direction toward a successful completion of that goal.

After all these years and everything that happened, I still believe that God used my encounter with Mariella at the alternative school and those teddy bears at the CACDC to lead me in my desire to fight for a state law to protect the innocent before they become victims.

For so long it felt like just a dream, or maybe a vision. I didn't acknowledge my feelings to anyone, but now it was happening. I gradually considered myself a woman determined to follow my mission wherever it led.

Mr. Leal and others said it would be a long journey, and that trusted people may fail me along the way. There was no real security except Christ, and I was totally convinced He would stick by me, no matter what.

In all honesty, I didn't have a clue where to start. So, I took Dad's advice and relied on the computer and telephone. My first objective was to learn if there were any existing laws addressing teacher and student education dealing with sexual abuse. From my own experience there were none. I was privileged to attend both public and private schools and had not ever heard the words "child sexual abuse" until after I was unfortunate enough to be groomed by an expert.

The computer divulged the names and numbers needed, and it was time to get some straight answers from real people. I called the Children's Advocacy Centers of Texas (CACTX), the Regional YMCA, and some local independent school districts first. I asked them all the same question: "Do you know if there is any sort of state requirement to implement educational training on child sexual abuse for students or teachers?" The answers from the other end of the line varied from a surprised, "Ahh . . . , I don't think so," "Do you mean sex education?," or, "Not to my knowledge," which all added up to nothing—I needed some facts.

My last call went to the Texas Education Agency (TEA). The first person I contacted seemed puzzled, if not a little suspicious, but she was gracious enough to say, "Please hold while I find someone who may be able to answer your question."

I waited until I was ready to push the "off" button and try another number when a voice on the other end said, "Thank you for waiting. I talked to some people who'd have this kind of information, and they're pretty sure there is no such law in place in the state of Texas."

That was the answer I needed, but looking back on that moment of truth, I still wonder if that was the answer I wanted to hear. I received it with a sinking heart and a sense of exhilaration at the same time. After all I had been through and personally witnessed from other children, the reality of the general public acknowledging child sexual abuse seemed non-existent. Or maybe it was such an unspoken, vile act it wasn't considered proper conversation among decent, "God fearing" people.

Contrasted with all these emotions, my whole body and soul had been conditioned to write my own guidelines about how to help protect children from sexual abuse, and I desperately wanted to see these guidelines put into action.

The school year at UTD and my internship at the center were coming to a close, but I still had a burning desire to find a way, or ways, to protect the innocent. Without prioritizing either objective, I wanted to give my full attention to both school and protecting children.

I'm not sure what I expected, but learning that not one single agency or organization had a required program in place to educate children, teachers, or parents on how to prevent or even recognize the symptoms of sexual abuse was disappointing to say the least. I was overwhelmed with the knowledge that this type of abuse was so widespread with almost no organized efforts to control or prevent it.

Fear gripped my youthful heart and skepticism surfaced as I realized that my meager understanding of the political system, coupled with only three years of college, was not enough preparation to face the world of politics. I told myself that hundreds, if not thousands, of people with less enthusiasm sponsored bills that were passed and approved by congress. I had friends, Mr.

Leal, and, most of all, Mom and Dad supporting my efforts and that should be enough, I finally reasoned.

When I got myself together after my frustrations from talking with so many agencies and organizations, it was time to go to work again. But, to be sure, I wanted to go over everything again with my closest confidant, Mom.

It was about six o'clock on a Friday night when Mom came through the door, looking like she was a lone survivor of a train wreck. This was the way she usually looked at the end of a week after teaching fifth-grade reading to about sixty kids at her school. After our initial greeting, I mentioned I had something important to discuss with her. "Honey, let's talk now. Your Dad went to pick up some dinner, but he won't be back for another half hour."

We rushed to my room and I shut the door behind us. Mom sat in my study chair, looked at me, and smiled. It occurred to me at that moment that Mom was always smiling when she looked at me, unless I was crying, or just sad about something. Anyway, she never interrupted me while I named all the agencies and organizations I had called. I told her about the conversations, while she maintained a slit of a smile as if she already knew the answer. I paused my monologue for about five seconds to catch my breath, and Mom couldn't take it any longer.

"Well . . . what did you find out?" Her face got serious.

"What I found out is at least as far back as Monday, December 29, 1845, there is no record of any law in the state of Texas that requires prevention training for public school students or teachers on child sexual abuse."

"Wish I could say I'm surprised, Honey. I've taught in both private and public schools for twenty years, and as far as I'm aware, not one teacher ever raised the question. It just seems to be a subject no one is comfortable discussing. It's something that happens to other people and is rarely mentioned in company."

I heard the garage door open, and slid off my perch on the bed. "Food is here," I heard Dad call. "Mom, I have about a thousand questions to ask—later. Will you be close to home tomorrow?"

"I'll be here, and maybe we can go somewhere for lunch."

Later that week, I talked to Mr. Leal about my time spent contacting various agencies about existing state laws. He was pleased with my work and told me so, saying, "I've already contacted a senator about it, and he has agreed to meet with us here at the center next week." Dan (we're on a first name basis now) mentioned that when we toured the center together, he would supplement what I said in my "pitch" with statistics. With three days to prepare my notes before our scheduled meeting, I couldn't wait. When the time came I had pages of notes. My only concern was how interested the senator would be on the topic.

Dan introduced the senator who, without saying another word, asked for a tour of the center. Together, we walked the senator through all the rooms and offices while Dan explained the services offered to children and families. As we moved along, I explained how I received services at the CACDC as a survivor, and later volunteered to intern there during my senior year of college. Upon hearing my remarks, he stopped and facing me said, "That takes a lot of courage."

As we continued to walk, he seemed to become more attentive, observing and commenting on the colorful painted wall murals.

When we reached the conference room at the end of the tour, I felt for my notes in my purse, only to discover I had left them in my car. In a panic, I wanted to crawl right under the conference table but then suddenly realized that wasn't a reasonable option. Instead, under my breath I prayed a quick prayer for guidance and help. A few seconds later, I was grounded again.

I clasped my hands together, set them on the table, and leaned forward a little. "Some children grow up being abused and it continues for years," I started. Then I paused long enough to move my left hand to my lap and sit up straight. Now, I was looking right at him while noticing a slight nod to his head. "Especially children need to be taught true boundaries and that it's OK to tell." I had my courage and confidence back now, and didn't need any notes—I had been there—lived that life for too long.

I explained that I had made some calls and asked if there were any laws on the books in Texas to require teacher or student education about child sexual, and other, abuse. "So far," I said, "from all the state and local agencies I've contacted, not one person in those offices seemed to know of any such requirement."

He thought about it and then suggested it was probably a good idea to consider some legislation. He said he would get back with me on the matter. I understood his last comment, and body language, to mean that maybe I had said enough. But I wasn't through explaining yet. There was so much more.

"Sir, a lot of the children's advocacy centers have tried to get into the schools to do these trainings. Because the training isn't required, some schools refuse to allow the training. All students can receive age-appropriate education that is on their level with these trainings." I was hurrying, now. Our time was limited and I knew Dan had plenty to add. I stopped and looked across at Dan and caught his thin-lipped smile.

Dan spoke with ease and authority, with maybe some urgency thrown in. "Prevention is the only way we're going to see the numbers go down," he said. The senator continued to listen and expressed a mild interest before reiterating that he was on a tight schedule. He thanked us for our time and repeated that he would be in touch and to contact his assistant if we needed anything else. We never heard from the senator again, and I am no longer embarrassed to admit I still can't remember his name.

After he left, Dan and I sat back in our chairs for a few seconds, both looking straight ahead. I was reflecting upon what really just transpired. I couldn't read Dan's mind, but for my part I didn't consider our meeting as a "winning" moment.

Dan finally broke the short silence without much lift to his voice. "He might not be the one for the job, but we'll just have to wait and see."

Shrugging my shoulders I said, "Well, it's important we align ourselves with someone who is really passionate about this issue." Moving on, I shared my list of legislators with Dan from the research I had compiled at home. Together we discussed other people who might be good candidates, and we agreed to continue looking. We both believed that one of the local representatives might be a good fit. State Representative Tan Parker, representing District 63 and Denton County, was our first choice.

Dan was quick to contact Representative Tan Parker's office and arrange to get on his schedule. After a few weeks (which felt like months), we got a tour of the CACDC on the books.

Our time to meet, once again, was at 3:00 p.m. on Wednesday the following week. I met with Dan at 2:50 p.m. to discuss the plans again for the tour. At 3:15 p.m. my heart sank into my chest when I thought he might not show. Then, he called the center to tell us that he was running behind, but that he would be there. He also mentioned he was bringing his wife with him. I was ecstatic—a woman's view—someone with whom I could feel really comfortable. I wasn't disappointed.

When Mr. and Mrs. Parker walked into the CACDC building, Dan and I greeted them at the door. "Hi, Dan," Representative Parker said, with a firm handshake. They had met before.

Dan then looked at me with a friendly smile and said, "This is Jenna Quinn, the intern who's got us all stirred up." Representative Parker extended his hand, wearing a friendly smile.

He then introduced his wife, Beth. She was stunningly beautiful. Her charisma and beauty filled the room. I felt instantly comfortable around both of them. *This is going to be a good day,* I thought.

Dan led the way for the tour. As the tour progressed from room to room, Tan and Beth Parker pelted Dan with questions. Beth showed herself to be a true professional, asking all the right questions, and seemed genuinely interested in learning how the center worked. I felt a strong connection with Beth as more and more I could feel her heartfelt interest.

At some point in the tour, Beth Parker spoke about her family. She said they had two little girls and went on to give us a warm and personal account of their interests and activities. At this point, they both knew I was a survivor. Beth asked me to speak about my experience at the center—"If you feel comfortable in doing so," she added. Her request gave me the opening I was waiting for but had not expected to get until we arrived at the conference room. Originally I planned to tell my story at the end of the tour, after they saw the entirety of the center. But after Dan looked my way with a smile and nodded approval, I couldn't wait.

I started out slowly but with full confidence. "I came in here through the same doors that all these children enter—hurt, broken, and confused, grasping for help and without much hope. Through the love, compassion, understanding, and guidance provided me by the counselors and others at the center, I was given the opportunity to start my recovery. I can't begin to tell you the miracles this center worked for me, and the miracles I've seen worked on other children." I had talked enough and didn't want to distract from anything else Dan had to say. After clearing my throat, I said, "That's all for now. My personal story will come later—maybe by way of a book." They all smiled and nodded.

The tour progressed in an unhurried fashion along the hallway. It got quiet after my last comments. I sensed they were waiting for more and I didn't want to disappoint them. I let it all out right then and there. "At every grade level, children should be reminded how to spot the warning signs of sexual abuse, and teachers should be taught both behavioral and emotional symptoms."

I paused for a few seconds, thinking Dan would speak next. It got quiet again, and it seemed everyone's focus was still directed at me. They wanted to hear more. Continuing my monologue, I said, "The school atmosphere provides a safe medium against blame when crying out for help because many times the person carrying out the harmful act is living in the same household.

"Looking back on my own experiences with it, I have to believe my childhood years would've been much different if I were given the opportunity at my school to make an outcry from the very beginning of the grooming process, before the damage was done.

"At the very least, I wouldn't have lived my life in a half-world-of-horror for so long. Court records indicate everything started when I was thirteen, but looking back, I can recognize the grooming started earlier, and I finally made my outcry when I was sixteen-years old." There was much more, of course, but I didn't want to take anything away from Dan. I said what I came to say, and much more than I anticipated.

The body language and silent expressions by both Tan and Beth Parker said it all. My spirits soared. Before the tour was half finished I relaxed knowing that we all had shared interests—a real partnership for whatever obstacles lay in our path.

When it was Dan's turn to share his thoughts, he reiterated much of what I had already said, adding that he and all his staff were 100 percent behind my efforts to work with legislators and propose a bill to incorporate measures allowing sexual abuse prevention into classrooms.

Visibly moved, Representative Parker said, "That's really great, and I think that is something I can help with. Let's schedule a time to get together again because I want to hear more and see if this is something we can do."

As the tour ended and we were all walking toward the exit, I was almost shivering with excitement and expectations. Representative Parker's last words were: "I'm very impressed with what you're doing here and your dedication to this cause. Do you have anything else to add?"

"I do have more ideas on what the bill could include."

"Great, please feel free to write, email, or call my office about anything."

Dan and I thanked them for coming, adding that I would contact them soon. The door barely closed when Dan turned to me and said, "Can you believe that?"

I felt a widespread smile across my face. "They are amazing, and it couldn't have gone any better." I let that moment sink in, with the secure feeling that something was really going to happen. But, at that time, even in my wildest dreams, I couldn't have pictured the tremendous amount of work needed for our plan to move any further off the launching pad.

CHAPTER 28

After meeting with Representative Parker, I couldn't wipe the half-smile from my face. That evening while telling Mom and Dad about our meeting, I could see excitement building in their demeanor as my story unfolded. When they settled down enough to comprehend the situation, I detailed as much as I could remember of what transpired with Representative Parker and his wife, Beth.

"He really seems to understand your heart for this cause," Mom said as she smiled.

"That was my prayer, too."

On Saturday morning I sat down with my morning cup of coffee and emailed Representative Parker, thanking him for his time and interest in furthering the cause. His reply arrived a few days afterward, saying he wanted to meet with me to get some things down on paper. Through a few more emails, we agreed to meet at the CACDC with Dan. This was a convenient place to meet since my internship was at the CACDC facility, which was close to Representative Parker's district office.

A few weeks later, Dan, Representative Parker, and I met in the CACDC conference room to discuss and plan our next step. Parker opened by saying he had some ideas on where to start. I hung on his every word. Throughout our discussion he remained optimistic that such a bill was needed and would strike a strong note with the other legislators. "With the timing of this, I think it could work out," he said. Then he looked at me and continued with a more serious tone in his voice, "Jenna, this is going to be your bill, so what are some of the things that you want to see?" I could barely control my excitement as I brought out my prepared notes.

His question really put me on the spot—just where I wanted to be. I was ready. "Training students and teachers for kindergarten through twelfth grade should be mandatory in all Texas schools. Also, schools should offer information to parents on how to recognize the signs and symptoms and other actions leading to sexual abuse, like grooming."

Continuing my monologue I asked that available counseling options be given to students who make an outcry after they have been harmed. "Kids that have been through this need to know they have somewhere to go for help." Representative Parker nodded his head and made some notes.

Dan also mentioned that the signs and symptoms are displayed differently across gender and age. Adding to Dan's response, I also explained that age-appropriate training should be included in the bill.

Parker stopped writing and commented, "You seem to know how you want this to look. I'm going to do the best I can to see that all your requests are met." Trying to contain my excitement, I thanked him again. We agreed the language of the bill would be drafted at our next meeting.

After our discussion, I tried not to get my hopes up too high. I knew very little about proposing a bill, lobbying, or much of anything else about what goes on at the State Capitol.

Representative Parker assured me that he was definitely going to do everything in his power to see this bill successfully passed by the Texas legislature. From my very first impression of Representative Parker, I accepted his word as gold. That was the kind of man he was, and still is.

Representative Parker agreed to write the language of the bill, but he didn't mention a time line. My impatience grew with the long wait, fearing some unforeseen circumstance would delay this important next step. Since my dream of passing the bill was in its infancy, I didn't mention it to anyone except my parents. Passing some form of legislation to get schools involved in protecting children from sexual abuse had become the center of my life, and it was a sacred cause to me.

As the weeks passed, Dan sensed my anxiousness and reminded me on several occasions, "Jenna, just be patient. Tan will keep his promise."

Dan's words still ring in my ears as I think about that period of anxiety. Finally, after a very long month (for me, at least) of waiting, all of our schedules came together for a meeting. Representative Parker came prepared with a hard copy of the language for the first draft, written on paper in the form of a House Bill.

After reading over his draft of the bill, I sat back in awe. Everything I had asked for and more was in the draft. When Representative Parker was sure he had my attention, he said, "Now Jenna, if this goes to the next stage, you will need to appear before the Texas House Committee on Public Education for a personal testimony."

"A testimony?"

He explained that testifying from personal experience would help give the bill purpose and meaning. "Do you think that's something you can do?" I felt caught off guard. This was the first time he mentioned anything about giving a testimony. Without pausing for too long, I said, "If that's what it takes to get this through, then of course I can do that."

"OK, good," he said. "We are going to need it. Have you ever been to the Capitol?"

Starting to laugh, I said, "No, I haven't. I'm not even sure what the building looks like, but I'm sure it will be a memorable first trip."

At our next meeting, Representative Parker had some disappointing news. He explained that we had to present the bill during the next legislative session, still a year away. My heart sank. To me, next year seemed about as far away as Christmas to a five-year-old child, and it must have shown on my face.

Representative Parker picked up on my mood. "It's going to work out. Don't worry. We are not in session this year, and it gives us time to prepare."

I nodded my head to agree but felt a sinking feeling inside. Since the timing was completely out of my control, I had no choice but to trust what he said. We agreed to stay in touch and run at full speed with the bill for the next session.

Meanwhile, I decided to focus on maintaining my grades and finishing the semester. My hard work in school led to good grades by the end of the school year, and almost before I realized it summer was upon me—a very long summer as it turned out. As the hot summer months passed, I hardly realized the giant stride we had made toward prevention.

During the summer I spent as much time as I could in prayer and fasting, praying for God to use my pain for good: "Lord, please take my experience and use it to help others. If this bill is your will, then let it be done quickly. See my heart and know that I am trying to do what I can to help others, but if this is coming from a selfish place, and not something you have put in my heart to do, then show me another way."

On a family trip to Colorado that summer, I confided in my Grandpa Boykin while at his ranch. I told him about what I experienced in that small waiting room with my parents after my SANE examination, and how that little pamphlet affected me. I explained that statistics showed one out of three girls and one in six boys in Texas, and probably elsewhere, experienced some kind of sexual abuse before the age of eighteen, and how unthinkable it was to know it was all there in one little room— mostly hidden from the general public, on one sheet of paper for any reasonable parent, teacher, or friend to read and recognize the symptoms.

I won't ever forget his reply.

He took off his worn cowboy hat and scratched his head before placing it back on his head. Finally, in his unhurried way, said, "Heck, without even doing the simple math, that's pretty near enough little kids to fill the whole Panhandle of Texas— and maybe enough left over to fill one of your fancy suburbs."

Grandpa was raised on a cattle and sheep ranch in Wyoming. He graduated from the University of Wyoming with a degree in agriculture and served in a professional capacity with the USDA (along with his own ranching activities) for most of his adult life.

But, if you got to know him well, it was easy to tell he never really left his Wyoming cowboy lingo far behind—straight and simple. Grandpa and I always shared a special relationship. He never failed to come up with something to make me smile or laugh, no matter how serious or light the subject.

I registered for my last semester of college in August and graduated in December 2008. After completing three and a half years of undergraduate school, I graduated cum laude from the University of Texas at Dallas with a bachelor of arts degree in psychology. On graduation day, my heart swelled with a sense of accomplishment, which was reflected by praise from my parents and all of my immediate family members who made the trip from out of town.

In January 2009, almost immediately after graduating, I accepted a part-time teaching position in the Psychology Department at UTD as a teaching assistant under the leadership of a tenure professor. My responsibilities were centered on helping declared psychology majors statistically design their research projects. I also accepted a job working full-time with autistic children, assisting in a method for therapy called Applied Behavioral Analysis.

Meanwhile, Representative Parker was working hard on the bill, and we talked often to keep it in motion. The legislative session began in January 2009 and Representative Parker officially filed the bill as House Bill 1041 in early February. While at work one afternoon I received an unexpected call from him. My heart leaped with excitement as we discussed the details of the bill.

"We have to move fast on this," he urged, explaining that, depending upon circumstances, I might need to make a hurried trip to Austin.

He informed me that he would propose H.B. 1041 in front of the House Public Education Committee "very soon," stressing that I should be ready at a moment's notice.

I didn't completely understand how the political process worked, but his message was plain enough. Before our conversation concluded, I was already thinking through what to pack and couldn't focus on anything else for the rest of the day.

State Representative Tan Parker hard at work.

Two days later, I received another call at work from Representative Parker. "Can you be here tomorrow? We need you to testify before the Public Education Committee. We don't know the time yet, but if you can be here in the morning, we'll be ready to go when the opportunity presents itself." Once a bill is filed, it's very difficult to predict when a bill will be scheduled for a hearing.

After giving my verbal agreement I hurriedly hung up the phone. Finally, after contacting my supervisor who approved a one day leave without pay, I called Mom to see if she could go with me for moral support. Mom taught all day and couldn't always answer her phone, so I called her five times before she picked up. "Honey, what's going on? Is everything OK?"

"Mom, I have to go to Austin to testify tomorrow. I plan to go even if you can't make it, but it would be great if you could come. Please come! This is so exciting!"

"I can't believe it's tomorrow. I wouldn't miss it for the world," she said. That evening over dinner we discussed our plans to travel to the Capitol. We had to drive in the morning and be back home that evening, so we could work the following day—seven hours behind the wheel.

Before bedtime, Mom stepped into my room and in her motherly tone of voice said, "I'd really love the chance to testify before the committee to speak, not only as a concerned parent, but as a teacher with experience in the classroom."

"That's a great idea, Mom." We hugged each other goodnight and then tried to get to sleep early. That evening as I said my prayers I thanked God for Mom's bravery and support. What happened the next day I shall never forget.

CHAPTER 29

When Mom and I arrived at the Texas State Capitol Building in Austin on April 21, 2009, I stood for a moment at the bottom of the steps to one of the entrances, staring with awe at the beautiful architecture.

Upon entering the building I was immediately lost. I knew Representative Parker's phone number but didn't have directions to his office. Thank goodness a security guard put us on the right course. We walked, and we walked some more, with me regretting at every step my choice to wear heels.

As we cruised through the corridors, a thought flashed through my mind: *If I were here to testify to a gathering of such an influential audience on any other subject, I would be shaking like an aspen leaf in October.* I wasn't nervous—I was looking forward with purpose to finally verbalizing the urgent need for a legal stop or dramatic slowing of child sexual abuse. I could hardly wait.

When we found Representative Parker's office, we were greeted with warm smiles. They were waiting for us. Mom had no problem expressing how excited she was to be there. Instead of shaking hands with the staff, she greeted everyone with a full-body hug.

The office legislative aid did her best to make us feel comfortable. "Please have a seat and make yourself at home. Would you like some water or coffee?"

While shifting around to find a seat, I said, "Water would be great, please."

Representative Parker sat down with us to explain that we were on standby for the day. "It may be a long day," he added, "but that's how things work around here." Then he looked at Mom and said, "Jenna mentioned in one of our previous conversations you would be willing to testify."

"I would be delighted," she said.

"Then, it's all set. We will sign up for time at the podium, and see how it goes from there."

I was never considered a "just sit and wait person." After pacing the room a few times, Representative Parker picked up on my actions by offering a solution.

"Would you all like to tour the Capitol?" he asked, with a knowing smile.

That was all the invitation we needed. "Well, if you don't mind. It's such a beautiful building," I said.

"Just please be sure to keep your phone on you," he said.

I smiled, reassuring him I would check my phone every minute.

As Mom and I strolled through the State Capitol, we got hungry for lunch. Since I had not heard anything yet, we walked back to the office to check in. Representative Parker's staff once again apologized for the wait and recommended that we go enjoy lunch. We found a little sandwich shop tucked into one of the Capitol corridors and enjoyed a quick meal.

After lunch, we toured some more and bought a few things in the souvenir shop. At this point, my feet were killing me from walking in high heel shoes. We decided to go back to the office and sit until we were needed.

I was checking the time again on my phone and making a mental note at the late hour of five o'clock when the door to Representative Parker's office opened and his legislative aid stood in the open door, smiling. "It's showtime everybody," she said.

Even though we waited all day, the reality of the moment still surprised me. But I was ready—more than ready, as the three of us (Representative Parker, Mom, and I) trailed toward the hearing room. As we walked, Representative Parker gave me an overview of what to expect, but five minutes later his instructions became a blur. I couldn't remember one word. Thinking back on it on the way home, I remembered my mind going blank, without one thought—not even thinking about my notes or whatever other impromptu information would be necessary to get my message across. I was ready, and there was just no more room for any more incoming directives.

When we finally stepped foot into the room, I captured a visitor's view of the layout—it was packed. I felt my spirits lift when I saw Dan seated with CACTX Executive Director Joy Rauls. Also with them was Madeline McClure, founder and CEO of TexProtects, a statewide organization for policy, advocacy, and prevention of child abuse. They all drove on a last minute notice to support the bill. Joy even signed up to testify before the committee to express support on behalf of the CACs across the state. In a heartfelt tone of voice, Joy looked at me saying, "Jenna, this is such an important opportunity for public education, and if there's anything else we can do to help, please let us know."

As we stood waiting (I couldn't guess for what), a man in a dark suit and tie approached Representative Parker and spoke a few words, none of which I heard.

Parker motioned to follow him out into the corridor. "I'm sorry," he said, without hesitation. "The Committee is behind schedule, and there might not be time on the agenda for your testimony."

I felt fainthearted and quietly excused myself to get some water, trying my best to keep it together. Then Representative Parker went back into the room and had some words. When he returned to meet Mom and me standing outside the room, he was smiling as he approached us. "Those are a bunch of nice folks," he said. "I only had to remind them once that you had traveled hours to be here, and that you had waited all day in my office for an opportunity to speak. You will get your chance," he concluded.

We were rushed to the meeting room, where I took my seat in the first full row of chairs up front and made a conscious effort to make eye contact with every committee member. Representative Parker spoke first. I was on the edge of my seat listening to him speaking eloquently on the merits of passing statewide legislation to protect children from sexual abuse. He spoke persuasively, with vigor. He explained how teachers are the primary reporters for child abuse cases and that "prevention is the answer."

Mom was scheduled next to testify but the Chairman called for me. My feelings of being caught off guard were overpowered by my eagerness to speak. I wasn't particularly nervous, but my whole body tingled with anticipation. I jumped up and only took a few steps, stopped in front of the podium, set my paper down, and grabbed each side of the podium with my hands.

What I prepared ahead of time was short and to the point. Leaning into the podium microphone to speak, I thanked the committee for hearing me. Then I stated I was there to represent and be a voice for the millions of children suffering from sexual abuse who currently didn't have a voice. "Right now, Texas has the unique opportunity to empower parents, teachers, and, most importantly, children to obtain the knowledge and skills necessary to enable victims to make an outcry."

Most importantly, I stated that I never received an opportunity to make an outcry or seek help at school because there were no laws to give children the information needed to get help. "We all know abuse is wrong," I said. Then I shared how children who are abused need to be reminded that it's a crime, it isn't their fault, and that it's OK to tell. I explained how my own parents and teachers, who knew me well, could not figure out what was wrong with me because they were never taught how to recognize the symptoms of sexual abuse.

"I am here for a simple reason." I asked the committee not to say "no" to giving children the information needed to prevent abuse and the *chance* to receive help. I put more into it than I thought I had in me. I left the podium, feeling very upbeat, and my adrenaline didn't subside when I sat down. The Chairman smiled, thanked me for speaking, and called Mom to the podium.

She walked to the podium as if she owned the stage—a practiced movement, as if she had done this every day of her life. Then Mom spoke from the perspective of a teacher and a parent. Together, with other important points, she stressed that every day sexual abuse goes undetected in the classroom.

She mentioned how she took me to see different doctors, looking for a diagnosis, but they couldn't find a cause for my symptoms other than stress. Then she described the moment she read the pamphlet in the hospital waiting room. "Parents, teachers, and students need knowledge to empower them to tackle and not avoid the issue of sexual abuse."

Joy Rauls testified next and discussed the importance of prevention training in schools and the curriculums available, then offered the services of the CAC as a resource. She was a confident lady, and her confidence was reassuring.

Representative Parker gave the closing statement, saying the bill was a "commonsense solution."

Before the committee closed the hearing, the Chairman thanked me for testifying and stated the bill was left pending. In less than twenty minutes, our hearing on the bill was over. Mom squeezed my hand so tight when we started for the door that I thought my fingers would break. Representative Parker thanked me over and over again for having the courage to testify before the committee. Emotionally drained is not a strong enough word for how I felt, but I was also relieved that my voice was finally heard.

Back in Representative Parker's office after the hearing, he explained that now the committee would debate whether or not the bill should go before the Texas House of Representatives for a vote. He assured us that he would keep me informed each step of the way. I thanked him for the opportunity, and then we said our good-byes.

Totally exhausted, Mom and I wiggled our way into our car seats for the long drive home. It had been a long day. During the journey, Mom and I carried on a nonstop dialogue for nearly two hours. At some point in our conversation, Mom said one sentence that still sticks with me: "Honey," she said, "you've come from almost being committed to a mental institution to telling your story at the State House. Is that surreal, or what?"

When our conversation slowed, I leaned back in the seat, closed my eyes, and quietly thanked God for His loving influence in making this day one that I could think back on as the start of something very special.

CHAPTER 30

Aweek after delivering my testimony to the Texas House Public Education Committee, Representative Parker contacted me. He said the committee agreed to move the bill forward. I wanted to jump up and down and shout for joy right there at work. He thanked me again and said my testimony was the driving force behind their decision to take the next step. I was grateful, while prayerfully holding my expectations in check.

With a favorable vote from the House Public Education Committee, the bill still needed a majority of votes from both the House of Representatives and the Senate and, finally, Governor Perry's signature was needed to make it a law. From our frequent phone conversations, it was evident Representative Parker was keeping the bill at the forefront of his discussions with his colleagues in Austin. However, this all seemed a world away from my nervous anticipation back at home.

On May 7, 2009, Representative Parker called to give me an update: "The House of Representatives passed the bill today with a unanimous 146 yeas and zero nays. It's going to move forward."

"Really?" I almost screamed.

Shaking with joy, my thoughts ran rampant. *No one opposed it?* All I could do was thank Representative Parker. As I processed the news, I asked my next question, "So, what happens now?"

"Here's what's next, Jenna," he said. "The proposed bill will now go to the Senate, where it must complete a similar committee process and pass with a majority vote by the full Senate. It looks good, but I learned long ago not to try and outguess this body of government. Keep the faith, and I will call you as soon as I know something."

It wasn't long until Representative Parker called to update me on the bill's progress. The bill was referred to the Senate Education Committee and was scheduled to be considered at a committee hearing on May 21, 2009. Representative Parker had significant concerns with whether the Senate committee would pass the bill out so that it could be voted on by the full Senate.

I didn't understand much of what he said, but I knew it wasn't good. A strong feeling of disappointment came over me. My heart sank into my stomach, and I couldn't find the words to speak.

He must have sensed my shock because only a few seconds passed before he spoke again. "There is still a chance, Jenna. H.B. 1041 is just a number. The Senate Education Committee would like to name the bill after you."

"I don't understand," I replied.

"We could call it Jenna's Law. A name associated with the proposed legislation will make it stronger and more meaningful."

Throughout the long process of writing the bill, testifying and debating changes in the House, the thought of naming the bill after me never crossed my mind or came up in conversation.

What a huge decision! I was willing to do anything to make the bill pass, but at what cost? There would be no turning back if I agreed.

I said a silent prayer and asked God for guidance because if the proposed bill were named after me I would be widely identified as a victim and no longer selective in sharing my abuse. Everyone would know.

In less than a minute I had my answer. The whole purpose of the bill was to protect children from sexual abuse. If allowing my name to be associated with the bill would help to get it passed without waiting another year, then so be it.

"Are you still there?" Representative Parker asked.

"Yes, I would be honored to have my name associated with the bill." I could feel a heightened mood as a smile crossed my face—finally "a chance . . . a voice . . . yes!" That's all we wanted all along.

"Thank you, Jenna," he said, in a heartfelt tone of voice. "You are a courageous person. This is going to help so many kids."

On May 30, 2009, I received my next phone call from Representative Parker with a heavy heart. He explained that a bill simply dies when it runs out of time to be voted on before the end of the legislative session. Today was the deadline to pass legislation or appoint conference committees to resolve differences between the chambers. A record number of conference committees were working to resolve differences that year, and Jenna's Law was among them. "Our bill is simply running out of time because of all these debates."

I could sense the strain in his voice. He was fighting hard for Jenna's Law and deeply desired to pass this legislation. This was our last chance to see the bill through for the session, which would terminate at midnight in two days on June 1, 2009.

"Even if we miss the deadline, think about what a wonderful experience it will be for you. Please come if you can. You wouldn't want to miss it," he said.

"I wouldn't miss it for the world."

May 31, 2009, Mom and I made it to the Texas State Capitol around 9 o'clock in the morning, and Representative Parker greeted us in his office. He explained that the conference committee had resolved the differences between the two chambers' versions of the bill, and now we needed a majority vote from both the full House of Representatives and the full Senate. The full House of Representatives needed to vote again on the Senate Committee amendments, including naming it Jenna's Law. Then the full Senate would vote once more.

By late afternoon, we were ready to go to the House of Representatives Chamber for the voting. Most of the debates and conference committees had ended.

Mom, Representative Parker's staff, and I perched in the balcony overlooking the main floor to watch the voting process. Several other people observed the proceedings from the public audience area. Representative Parker was ready to present Jenna's Law on the House floor.

On the floor, the Representatives were sitting in their chairs, getting ready to vote. Other bills were presented and passed, or not passed. With each round of voting I felt myself getting more nervous by the minute. Some people in the audience directed their attention toward me with pleasing expressions, as if they recognized why I was present. Mom said, "Look, Honey, you seem to have support." I smiled and raised my hand slightly to acknowledge their attention.

When the Speaker of the House announced House Bill 1041, Jenna's Law, my whole body jerked. Representative Parker approached the podium and gave a description of the bill and the agreement made in the conference committee. The voting results were on the front wall of the room. A green light lit up for a yes vote and a red light lit up for a no vote.

Mom and I anxiously grasped each other's hands when the voting started. I took a deep breath but felt like I wasn't getting air. I watched carefully as the first few Representatives cast their vote. First a few green yeas lit up the voting board, then another wave of yeas popped up. Mom and I looked at each other with awe but didn't make a sound. She squeezed my hand even tighter. My body stiffened as my eyes focused on the House voting board and I braced myself for the end result. A few seconds later, more green yeas lit up the board. Then, more yeas came in. Mom couldn't take it. She gasped and in the same breath said, "That's it. I think that's enough for the majority." In a matter of seconds the voting was over.

There was a short pause before the Speaker of the House announced that Jenna's Law passed the House of Representatives unanimously with 145 yeas and zero nays. I was stunned. Before processing everything that was happening in that moment, Mom jumped up out of her chair on impulse, and Representative Parker rushed back to the podium in excitement to speak.

"This bill we just passed, as we refer to it as 'Jenna's Law,' was written with the help of Jenna Quinn, who is a very strong advocate and community leader for preventing child sexual abuse here in Texas. Thanks to her work, fewer children in Texas will find themselves victims of this horrendous crime in the future!"

He then looked up to the balcony where Mom and I sat and, while smiling ear-to-ear, directed the other representatives, "It is my great pleasure to recognize and welcome both Jenna as well as her mother Kellie Quinn . . . , would you please recognize them here today. This is their bill!"

As Representative Parker stood there, the other representatives on the floor swiveled in their leather-bound chairs, looked up at me, and clapped. *Was this real?* Fighting back tears, I acknowledged their applause with a wave.

I had never seen Mom so excited about anything—ever. "I can't believe it, oh my gosh, no opposing votes!" she repeated, holding both my hands and moving her body up and down as if preparing for a launch off the balcony. Then, after all her adrenaline was exhausted, she said, in an almost normal tone of voice, "Do you realize what you have done?"

Genuinely speechless, and after what was probably a minute or two, I quietly said, "I'm beginning to."

After the voting, I thanked Representative Parker's staff members who were in the balcony with us during the proceedings—they were enjoying their own private celebration before joining our fun. When Representative Parker showed, he spoke first.

"Well, you did it," were his first words.

On impulse I ran to him even before he was through speaking and threw my arms around him. Holding back tears, I said, "How can I thank you enough for all your hard work? I can't believe it."

He was smiling and said, "We both know how important this is. And you are the one we can thank for all your hard work and sacrifice."

We took pictures together, and Representative Parker introduced me to other legislators who wanted to greet me. I was truly humbled and at a loss for words.

We all went back to Representative Parker's office to talk and privately savor our victory. My adrenaline stayed high because the Senate vote was next. No matter the outcome, I knew Representative Parker, his staff, and I did the best we could.

The Senate voted, and when it was all said and done, the votes were in favor of Jenna's Law with 31 yeas and 0 nays. We were almost there. Representative Parker explained that Governor Perry still needed to sign the bill before it became law. He suggested my whole family come for the signing.

Before leaving his office, I thanked him and said, "You worked so hard to make all this happen, and I will never forget you."

On June 19, 2009, Governor Rick Perry signed Jenna's Law. My whole family, Mom, Dad, Lauren, Stephanie, and husband Daniel with baby Luke secure in his car seat, drove to the Capitol for a ceremony of the signing scheduled on August 25, 2009. As we waited in one of the Capitol corridors, we spotted Governor Perry and a few of his staff approaching. When they drew closer to us, Mom and the Governor made eye contact. That was enough for Mom. She raised a hand with a little wave and said, "Good morning, Governor Perry."

He walked right over to us, as if he had known us forever. With a big smile showing on his face, he said, "I'm so glad to see the whole family here today." He shook everyone's hand, and without further words, he said, "Are you guys ready? This is a special day. Let's get this bill signed."

After our short greeting with Governor Perry, my family went to Representative Parker's office where we visited a few minutes before we strolled as a group (my family, Representative Parker, and his personal staff) to the "Governor's Reception Room" in the Capitol Building. As we walked toward the designated signing room, Representative Parker offered a personal tour of the Capitol after the signing ceremony. He also mentioned, in casual conversation, that other representatives and senators wanted to attend the signing.

Governor Rick Perry and Jenna at the Jenna's Law signing ceremony at the Texas State Capitol in Austin.

Representative Parker introduced me to more senators and representatives than I could keep count. One senator greeted me and said, "Did you know that no other state has a school mandate like this that's named after a survivor? Texas has made history and I'm proud to be a part of it."

Camera crews and others with cameras took their positions as we all gathered around Governor Perry's desk. Governor Perry looked up at me and grinned saying, "I'm happy to do this." Then he picked up his pen and signed Jenna's Law. He froze for the camera, smiled, and then he handed me the signature pen. "Keep this as a reminder."

I stood staring at the pen in awe. It was the most beautiful pen I had ever seen.

"Thank you. I will keep it forever."

As the flashes of light from the cameras went off, I looked around the room. My family was there by my side. It was truly a celebratory moment for us. They were there for me, not only in the dark times, but also in the joyful moments. Fighting back tears of love and appreciation, I hugged and thanked my family and others involved for their perseverance and support.

After the signing, one of the senators gave me a big hug and said he flew there that day just to meet me. He put his hand on my shoulder and said, "You know, it's a miracle you didn't have to die for this law. Victims who have laws named after them are not usually around to see it."

"I just died in a different way," I replied. "But with God's help and incredible hard work from Representative Parker and others, I was restored to life to do something to prevent, not just treat, child sexual abuse."

My desire to pass Jenna's Law was not only to prevent abuse but also to glorify God by giving a voice to the voiceless. It wasn't about me. It was about God's redemptive power to save, heal, and restore those who are hurting. For too long I suffered in silence, was shackled by shame, and believed the painful lies that shame whispered to my soul. What I kept in secret and hidden in the dark had power over me. We can't heal what we don't reveal. But shame loses its power when it's exposed. Those who have been hurt by abuse need to know that they deserve to get help.

And regardless of what was done *to* them—they are pure in heart.

ACKNOWLEDGMENTS

No one writes a book alone. So it is time to say a thousand thanks to everyone who has been a part of writing this book.

My gratitude is endless to Janét McDaniel, my principal editor, who spent hours on making this book a reality and caring for its beating heart. Thank you for taking the time to get to know me personally, and for your expertise and dedication to this cause. It's truly been a joy to work with you.

Thank you to my grandfather, Dennis Boykin, for assisting me in writing this book. You are a true warrior at heart, and I am eternally grateful for your countless hours of help and tireless work. When you got involved, the real work began, and I saw my hopes for this book come to fruition.

A special thanks to my friend, Norma Jones, for editing the first draft of this book and for your constant expressions of approval and support.

I'm beyond grateful to have people who have helped me, not only in writing this book, but also in other ways:

A very special thanks to the unconditional love and unequivocal support of my husband, Michael. Thank you for allowing me to spend most of my time with the computer, for not letting me give up, and for bringing me copious cups of coffee as I sat and wrote for hours at a time. You are my rock.

To every single member of my immediate family, my thanks to you would be another book of its own. Mom and Dad, you have helped shape me into the woman I am today. Dad, I can always count on you for *anything*. Mom, thank you for spending hours reading through this book with me and for being my personal cheerleader in life. Stephanie and Lauren, you have both saved my life in different ways. I love you both immensely.

I have a very special thank you for my state prosecutors, Jeff Fleming and Debra Bender, along with Beverly Bailey, my victim intervention specialist, who stayed by my side during the trial. Thank you for the work that you do to bring justice and healing to those who have been hurt. I am eternally grateful for the justice I received.

I can't give enough thanks to everyone at the Children's Advocacy Center for Denton County that helped me through my healing process. Dan Leal, you are a friend forever. Rose Boehm, thank you for allowing me to "unravel" for hours in counseling and for your sense of humor.

Thank you to Texas State House of Representatives, Tan Parker, for your understanding of how important it is to address child sexual abuse and your courageous efforts in championing Jenna's Law. I am forever grateful.

RESOURCES

Childhelp—www.childhelp.org
Childhelp is a leading national nonprofit organization dedicated to helping victims of child abuse and neglect. Childhelp's approach focuses on prevention, intervention, and treatment.
Childhelp National Child Abuse Hotline: 1-800-4-A-Child (1-800-422-4453)

Childhelp Speak Up Be Safe Prevention Education Curriculum: Research-based, developmentally appropriate curriculum for pre-kindergarten through grade 12.

Childhelp Speak Up Be Safe helps children and teens learn the skills to prevent or interrupt cycles of neglect, bullying, and child abuse—physical, emotional, and sexual. The program uses an ecological approach to prevention education by providing materials to engage parents and caregivers, teachers, school administrators, and community stakeholders.

Darkness to Light—www.d2l.org
Darkness to Light's mission is to empower adults to prevent child sexual abuse. Their programs raise awareness of the prevalence and

consequences of child sexual abuse and educate adults to prevent abuse or intervene appropriately if abuse is suspected.

Darkness to Light Stewards of Children Training: This prevention-training teaches adults how to prevent, recognize, and react responsibly to child sexual abuse. The program is designed for individuals concerned about the safety of children as well as organizations that serve youth.

GRACE—www.netgrace.org

GRACE stands for **Godly Response to Abuse in the Christian Environment.** The mission of GRACE is to empower the Christian community through education, training, and consultations to recognize, prevent, and properly respond to child abuse. GRACE recently launched a comprehensive child safeguarding certification initiative for churches and Christian organizations.

National Children's Alliance—www.nationalchildrensalliance.org

National Children's Alliance (NCA) is the national association and accrediting body for Children's Advocacy Centers (CACs). NCA has been providing support, technical assistance, and quality assurance for CACs, while serving as a voice for abused children for more than twenty-five years. A children's advocacy center is a child-friendly facility in which law enforcement, child protection, prosecution, mental health, medical and victim advocacy professionals work together to investigate abuse, help children heal from abuse, and hold offenders accountable.

Biker's Against Child Abuse International (B.A.C.A.)—www.bacaworld.org

Bikers Against Child Abuse, Inc. exists with the intent to create a safer environment for abused children. This body of bikers empowers children to not feel afraid of the world in which they live. They stand ready to lend support to wounded friends by involving them with an established, united organization. They work in conjunction with local and state officials who are already in place to protect children. They are prepared to lend their physical and emotional support to children by affiliation, and their physical presence. They stand ready to shield children from further abuse.

World Childhood Foundation—www.childhood-usa.org
The World Childhood Foundation was founded in 1999 by Her Majesty Queen Silvia of Sweden with the mission to defend children's right to a happy and safe childhood, free from sexual abuse and exploitation. To date, the Foundation has provided support to over one thousand projects in more than twenty countries including the United States.

S/HE (Secure/ Higher Ed)—www.securehighered.com
A large and diverse group of professionals from multiple fields related to gender based violence created Secure/Higher Ed with a singular goal: find a way—any way—to reduce the sexual and relationship violence epidemic. After years of self-funded research directed at a multitude of possible solutions, it became clear that training students in grades 1 through college (and when possible their parents) in situational awareness, self-defense, and survivor compassion offered the best hope for a reduction in sexual assault and relationship violence. S/HE's consistently updated program is based on the latest pedagogical, psychological, and criminological research, plus extensive post-training surveys of participants and their parents.

ABOUT THE AUTHOR

 **Jenna Quinn** was seventeen years old when she spoke out publicly for the first time as a survivor of sexual abuse and has dedicated the last twelve years of her life to preventing sexual abuse. With a master's degree in communication studies, she enjoys personally connecting with sexual abuse survivors and building rapport with audiences, young and old. Jenna is eager to help victims heal and takes every opportunity to speak publicly in order to raise awareness.

At the age of twenty, Jenna moved into the political system and reached out to Texas legislators about the need for schools to adopt age-appropriate curriculum on child sexual abuse. Supporting the cause, Texas State Representative Tan Parker championed what is now known as Jenna's Law in May 2009. Jenna's Law passed the Texas State Senate unanimously, making it the first child abuse prevention education law in the United States named after a survivor.

In September 2011, Jenna's Law was expanded to reach additional public institutions and addresses both sexual abuse and other forms of maltreatment. Jenna is a sought-after speaker by law enforcement groups, nonprofit organizations, schools, communities of faith, and various abuse prevention and intervention groups. Jenna is sharing her message of hope to audiences all across the country.

As a former educator, Jenna Quinn is committed to the cause of preventing child abuse, raising awareness through education, and increasing awareness of God's presence, love, and grace. She has a passion for justice and social change to make the world a safer place for children. As an inspirational speaker she is transparent about her experience with sexual abuse, how it has impacted her life and her family, and her transforming journey to healing. Her firsthand accounts of the harsh realities of sexual abuse and the truth of its effects have captivated audiences and has the power to forever change the way society views abuse and its prevention.

Jenna lives with her husband, Michael, in Dallas, Texas.

To contact Jenna, visit her webpage: www.JennaQuinn.org

 Jenna's Law on Facebook

 @Jennas_Law on twitter